Koi

Koi

A handbook on keeping Nishikigoi

Servaas de Kock
Ronnie Watt

FIREFLY BOOKS

A FIREFLY BOOK

Published by Firefly Books Ltd. 2006

First printing

Publisher Cataloging-in-Publication Data (U.S.)
De Kock, Servaas.
Koi : a handbook on keeping nishkigoi / Servaas de Kock & Ronnie Watt.
[160] p. : col. photos. ; cm.
Includes bibliographical references and index.
Summary: Guide to keeping koi, including their anatomy and physiology, different varieties
and basic strategies of feeding and care for koi. Also covers the principles of pond design and
how to prepare for showing koi in competition.
ISBN-13: 978-1-55407-215-6 (pbk.)
ISBN-10: 1-55407-215-8 (pbk.)
1. Koi. 2. Fish ponds. I. Watt, Ronnie. II. Title.
639.3/7483 dc22   SF458.K64.D45   2006

Library and Archives Canada Cataloguing in Publication
De Kock, Servaas
Koi : a handbook on keeping nishkigoi / Servaas de Kock & Ronnie Watt.
Includes biliographical references and index.
ISBN-13: 978-1-55407-215-6
ISBN-10: 1-55407-215-8
1. Koi. I. Watt, Ronnie II. Title.
SF458.K64D44   2006 639.3'7483   C2006-901044-7

Published in the United States by
Firefly Books (U.S.) Inc.
P.O. Box 1338, Ellicott Station
Buffalo, New York 14205

Published in Canada by
Firefly Books Ltd.
66 Leek Crescent
Richmond Hill, Ontario L4B 1H1

Designer: Maryna Beukes
Design Concept: Elmari Kuyler
Illustrator: Steven Felmore

Printed in Singapore

Contents

Koi: past and present

Over the past few decades there has been an increased interest in koi-keeping, motivated, at least in part, by the fact that we spend more time in and around our homes. As a pastime, koi-keeping combines the nurturing qualities of a pet lover with the esthetic pleasure of enhancing the home and garden.

An appreciation for the culture and tradition of the East is also evident in the trend toward keeping quality koi of recognized varieties, and making an effort to meet their special needs.

Termed "living jewels," koi have enchanted their admirers for centuries and their popularity shows no sign of waning.

The history of koi-keeping

The fish we today know as koi are descendants of the common carp, *Cyprinus carpio*, which originated in Central Asia many millennia ago. From here, they spread westward into Europe and eastward into China, following the rivers and waterways, especially those that fed the great inland seas of the region: the Black, Azov, Caspian, and Aral.

Early humans, who cultivated carp for food, most likely introduced them to the region's many lakes and rivers, from where they migrated naturally over time. Carp fossils dating back 20 million years have been found in South China, suggesting that they are among the earliest forms of recognizable aquatic life.

Moving somewhat closer to the present, the word "koi" was first used in about 500 BC in China, in a book written about the breeding of carp, one of the earliest records of its kind. Buddhist lore has it that one of Confucius's sons was given a fish named Koi by King Shoko of Ro at his birth in 533 BC.

Although it is not known exactly when carp were introduced to Japan, it is likely that they were brought into the country either by Chinese invaders who settled and gradually merged their own culture with that of their new homeland or via the many trade caravans that traversed the Orient. There is documented evidence of carp in Japan from about 31 BC and by AD 250 there are mentions in Japanese manuscripts of red-,

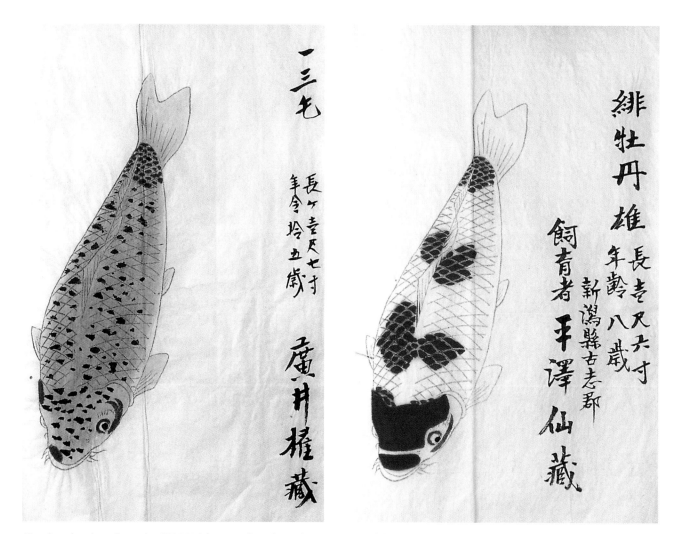

Catalog drawings from the 1915 Taisho Expo in Tokyo. The Japanese writing gives the owner's details, as well as the type of fish, its size, age, nickname, and the price it was expected to fetch. Although no fish were sold at the expo, they generated interest and some were presented to the new Emperor after young Prince Showa expressed a fascination with the colored fish.

white-, and blue-colored carp. (Another belief is that colored carp originated in China between AD 700 and 1000 and were being exported to Japan by 1500.)

The first signs of the modern era of koi-keeping began in the 19th century, in the region of present-day Niigata Prefecture, on the west coast of the main Japanese island of Honshu. Here, local farmers bred carp (*magoi*) to supplement their diet of rice. In an early example of mixed farming, the carp were raised in the ponds that were used to flood the rice paddies.

When color mutations appeared, it wasn't long before these carp were separated and bred on purpose. A red mutation (*hoo-kazuki*) was found first, followed by a white mutation. Cross-breeding eventually resulted in red and white carp (called *hara-aka* or *hara-hi*, meaning "red belly").

As the interest in this pastime grew, further selective breeding, which took place in the region now known as Yamakoshi, produced the *Sarasa*, a carp with a white body and red markings on its back, the true ancestor of the most-prized of all koi, the *Kohaku*, a white-bodied carp with various red markings on its head, back, and flanks (see page 36).

The modern era

In Japan, colored carp became known as "koi" (or "goi" when used as part of a word). From the Meiji era (1867–1912) to the middle of the Taisho era (1912–1926), koi were variously referred to as *Moyogoi* (koi with patterns), *Moyomono* (thing with patterns), or *Kawarigoi* (fancy patterns). *Irogoi* (colored koi) was another name in use in Japan at that time.

Surprisingly, one of the principal lines of mutation did not have its genetic roots in Japan but halfway across the world, in Austria, where scaleless carp, known as leather carp (*kawagoi*), were bred in 1782, followed by mirror carp (*kagami-goi*), with large reflective scales, in 1798. These *doitsu* (German) carp were first imported into Japan in 1904 to supplement the breeding of carp as a food source. However, cross-breeding with fully scaled colored carp soon produced many beautiful variations of koi.

In the seventh year of the Taisho era (1919), Kiyoshi Abe, a prefecture government fisheries expert, saw a *Sanke* bred by Eizaburo Hoshino in Takezawa-mura and promptly dubbed it *Nishikigoi* in praise of the splendor of the fish. *Nishiki* means "beautiful color combination" and is specifically applied to the high-quality woven brocade used to create the waist belt (*obi*) worn with a kimono. It has become common today for koi to be known as "living jewels" or "swimming flowers," reflecting the esteem with which they are held in Japan.

One of the great genetic scoops in the development of modern koi was the breeding of the first true metallic variety, the *Ogon*. Takehira Hoshide, of Hoshide Nishikigoi Farm, tells how, in 1921, Sawata Aoki, a koi farmer from Yamakoshi village in Niigata, heard of a carp with streaks of gold on its dorsal fin that had been fished out of the river by a child in the neighboring county. Although it turned out to be nothing more than a wild carp with a shine at the base of the dorsal fin, Sawata nevertheless bought it and bred it.

Over time, he retained only those offspring that had a lot of golden color and bred them in turn. In 1946 he purchased a female *Shiro-Fuji* that he bred to eight of his own males. Among the fry were about 30 very interesting and unusual fry, totally unlike the parent koi. Of these, two developed into fish with their entire bodies clad in gleaming golden scales: the original *Ogon* koi (see page 61).

At the Taisho Expo, held in Tokyo in 1915 to honor the new Emperor Taisho, breeders from the impoverished Niigata Prefecture, who sought to promote trade in their fish, brought 33 of their prime examples to the show, transporting them in wooden barrels by train to the showgrounds. These fish created such a stir that eight of them were presented to the Imperial Court. The exhibition's success, plus the Japanese royal family's growing fascination with *Nishikigoi*, unlocked the market for the farmers of Niigata and, in time, breeding koi became a principal industry for the area.

As Japanese breeders continued to improve koi by selective breeding and to experiment with cross-matches to produce new color variations, the enjoyment of koi gained new converts in the West.

Koi-keeping today

Koi were first introduced into mainland North America in 1938, reaching Hawaii a year later, but it was not until after World War II, when commercial air travel became a reality and Westerners were able to travel more easily to China and Japan, that the hobby started to develop. As people began to encounter the "colored fish" for themselves, it wasn't long before both Japanese and European traders established the means to ship koi to Europe, the United States and elsewhere.

Koi were taken to Canada in 1949, and the first commercial importation of koi into the United Kingdom took place in 1966. From 1970 onward, koi-keeping blossomed in the West.

However, in the early stages, there was little interest in the esthetic of the varieties, with quantity being more important than quality. Most Western breeders imported small fish, more easily transported from Japan, growing them up for sale in their home countries, which helped to reduce the price.

In recent years, a major source of koi has been Israel, where commercial-grade fish are produced on kibbutzim. The ready availability of fish in substantial numbers has helped popularize koi-keeping in Europe and the United States, although enthusiasts still insist on Japanese-bred fish. Koi are also produced in Thailand, China, Malaysia, India, and South Africa.

Wherever koi are found, local and regional koi clubs, koi shows, magazines, the Internet, and a new breed of specialist

Koi enthusiasts gather around a fellow member's home pond. Koi appreciation societies can be found all over the world, a tribute to the extent to which these "living jewels" have found favor in the West.

dealers have further helped to promote awareness of what constitutes good koi. Credit must also be given to the ZNA (Zen Nippon Airinkai) for bridging the cultural gap through education campaigns, sending Japanese judges to officiate at shows, and training Westerners as koi judges.

As an international promoter of koi-keeping, based in Japan, the ZNA plays a valuable role in disseminating information through its affiliated clubs and societies around the world. There are 50 ZNA chapters in Japan, plus 44 chapters and six friendship clubs elsewhere in the world.

The ZNA organizes more than100 koi shows (competitions) per year within Japan and membership is compulsory for anyone with aspirations of becoming a ZNA certified judge.

Over and above the ZNA, there are more than 100 clubs in the United States and Canada with links to the AKCA (Associated Koi Clubs of America). Across Europe, koi clubs are active in many countries, with membership ranging from a few dozen to hundreds of enthusiasts.

Most local clubs meet on a regular basis to exchange ideas and engage in *koi dangi* (koi talk). They hold shows to compete among themselves; many publish newsletters to promote koi appreciation and supply members with information on a vast range of topics, from health care and pond maintenance to new products.

The landscaped koi pond forms an attractive feature of this garden. Depending on your level of enthusiasm and involvement, a pond may be regarded as an investment, or simply a focal point around which to relax and enjoy your home.

Koi bloodlines

The term "bloodline" is used to describe fish belonging to a specific type and variety, stemming from a particular pedigree, and which consistently display a sought after characteristic worthy of earning a distinguishing name for those fish.

Bloodlines are developed by systematic breeding through specific lines in order to promote a high incidence of favored characteristics in the offspring. It stands to reason that if you want to breed a fish with particular characteristics, you are more likely to achieve the desired result if you use parent fish in which the characteristics are inherent, rather than a random breeding of two fish with unknown genetic backgrounds.

Only two koi varieties have true bloodlines: *Kohaku* and *Sanke*, and these are much sought after. In all other varieties, breeders use breeding groups that have the capacity to produce specific traits, but with little certainty that the progeny will perpetuate the same qualities as the parents. However, if the characteristics of a bloodline are known, a koi-keeper can confidently predict how the fish will develop in terms of its inherent quality, provided, of course, that pond management is of the highest standard. Buying fish from long-established bloodlines has always been a safe bet, but nowadays the bloodline is not as important as the koi itself.

In Japan, during the Meiji era (1867–1912), breeders in Yamakoshi competed with each other to produce good quality *Kohaku*. In 1889, Kunizo Hiroi of Gosuke farm in Higashiyama village produced the *Gosuke-Sarasa*. Some of the Gosuke offspring were sold in the late 1890s to Jiemon who in turn supplied offspring to Genjiro. Gorobei obtained fish from Genjiro and in the early 1920s supplied offspring to Genii Hoshino whose koi farm was known as Tomoin. Manzo also obtained some of the Gosuke offspring via Genpachi.

Tomoin and Manzo may be called the first true *Kohaku* bloodlines because their koi founded successor bloodlines such as *Yagozen*, *Buketa*, *Sensuke*, *Sankuro*, *Hasegawa*, *Ogawa*, *Dainichi*, and *Sakai* (Hiroshima).

Kohaku, *like these* Torazo Kohaku *of the* Dainichi *bloodline, are highly prized and breeders will always try to bring out the best characteristics to enhance the gene pool of future offspring in the hope of raising a supreme champion.*

As regards *Sanke*, some tricolored fry were bred in 1914 by Heitaro Sato in Uragara from a *Kohaku* female and two *Kohaku* males. One of the males had two small black spots at the top of the rays on a pectoral fin. There was great interest in the fish and, spurred on by this, Heitaro repeated the breeding in 1915. However this produced only about 10 tricolored fry that looked anything like the earlier tricolored *Sanke*.

Heitaro then sold the breeding group to Chobei of Yamakoshi village who bred the parent fish once only and sold the group in 1917 to Eizaburo Hoshino of Takezawa.

Hoshino introduced a male *Shiro-Bekko* into the breeding group. The result was progeny with stripes (*shima*) on the fins, and they were therefore named *Shima Sanke*. Because it was a new variety produced during the Taisho era, people gave the fish the name *Taisho-Sanshoku* (in the written form, but pronounced *Taisho Sanke*). In the modern era of *Sanke*, the best known bloodlines are *Isumiya*, *Torazo*, *Jinbei*, *Sadazo*, *Kichinai*, *Matsunosuke*, and *Dainichi*.

Obtaining bloodline koi

Bloodline koi are limited, but there are dealers who specialize in providing koi of bloodline varieties. These dealers usually make buying trips to Asia to make selections from the ponds of agents of the famous breeders.

If you aspire to own a koi from a famous bloodline, or at least from a famed breeder, then consult a specialized dealer who will advise you of when and where he or she will be shopping for new koi. You can set a maximum price, but take into account that the dealer will add a commission, and there may also be shipping charges to pay. Sometimes the dealer will provide photographs of the fish reserved for purchase and you will be able to make a final selection, but more often you simply have to trust the dealer's expertise and judgment.

Investing in quality koi is not for the novice, as the fish are expensive; they may also be "unfinished" and it will require both patience and experience to develop their full potential.

While it can be hard to cull seemingly "normal" fish, a sincere breeder knows that precious pond resources are better utilized in nurturing a smaller crop of sound fry toward adulthood than raising a vast number of average fish with no real value.

Koi genetics

The dedication of many generations of Japanese koi farmers has given us the modern koi, with its more than 100 varieties and their distinctive color and pattern variations, some more sought after than others.

The qualities of koi, as enjoyed by keepers, breeders, and enthusiasts, are governed by an intricate set of genetic and environmental factors. The genetic (inherited) composition of a fish is called the genotype. The physical qualities observed are collectively known as the phenotype.

Until recently, the knowledge of koi genetics was limited and mostly unavailable to koi farmers. In the pioneering years of koi breeding, farmers had to rely on tradition and intuition to create and fix their lineages. Chance also played a role.

Modern koi breeders have wide access to scientific research. The study of genetics in general involves the study of visible traits in offspring. Using traditional methods, it typically takes 20 generations of dedicated, well-planned, selective breeding in order to establish traits of desired character in koi. Results need to be painstakingly recorded and that, sadly, is a tradition followed by very few, if any, traditional koi farmers.

Studies of koi genetics have been slow, because koi take around two to three years to reach maturity. Carp can mature in a much shorter time, but koi breeders have inadvertently slowed the rate at which fish reach maturity even further by breeding for improved body conformation in order to produce large, show-winning fish. They would never use a female developing gonads at the age of one year.

In recent years, improvements in analytical techniques for genome investigation have sped up genetic research. These techniques were applied particularly to studies done in 2001 into the genetic variability of the koi stock of Niigata's Yamakoshi region, where a relatively high mortality rate at the larval stage had been observed. Koi were obtained from all the major breeders in the region and analyzed. The study found that not only was there a low genetic variability within the Niigata population, but the genetic distance between *Kohaku*, *Sanke*, and *Showa* was small, indicating that these favored varieties must have originated from a small founding population.

In time, this could threaten the status of the Niigata koi stocks, since inbreeding results in the loss of gene diversity.

Breeders and koi-keepers try to select individual fish most likely to carry on the characteristic traits of their variety. This both strengthens the gene pool and improves the species.

Given that Niigata is the source of parent fish for serious koi producers all around the world, it is important that the gene pool remains strong.

Koi breeders often try to manipulate the genotype in an effort to breed high quality koi according to their own values and sense of appreciation. This could mean selectively breeding for better growth and body conformation, or improved skin, color, and pattern characteristics. They may even try to control environmental factors, such as pond water temperature, as far as possible in order to deliver perfect fish for the market.

Koi-keepers, on the other hand, may try to enhance the phenotype (see page 22) by masterminding spectacular pond environments and introducing calculated feeding regimes, including color enhancers. You should remember, however, that it is not possible to enhance the qualities of a koi that has poor genetic material in the first place. By contrast, it is easy, simply through poor koi-keeping, to destroy a fish that has good genetic potential.

Among the recent trends in genetic manipulation are attempts to produce new varieties, such as "green" and "purple" koi. "Green" koi, or Midorigoi, were first bred in the 1960s as a subvariety of *Kawarimono* (see page 56) and efforts are still in progress to produce a green variety that breeds consistently true. In many cases, however, the green tends to blacken with age.

In a similar vein, the search for a purple-colored koi, which has been going on for over 25 years, has seen breeder Yoshu Hirado, of Chiba Prefecture, produce *Shiryu* (purple-colored) and *Shiryu-shigure* (brown markings on a purple ground) from crossbreedings of *doitsu*, *Ogon*, and *Showa*.

A typical Japanese mud pond, where fry are reared in a natural, yet secure, environment. The feeding program, pond temperature, and water characteristics are instrumental in determining the growth and quality of adult fish.

Anatomy and physiology

Koi belong to the species *Cyprinus carpio*, the common carp, in the family Cyprinidae, the order Cypriniformes, and the class Osteichthyes. The scientific nomenclature describes it as a fish with a skeleton partly made of bone but without true spines in the fins, with abdominal pelvic fins, evenly curved-edge scales, a swim bladder linked to the inner ear, and three rows of pharyngeal teeth. Koi have a bony skeleton with a skull, spine, ribs, and other appendages. The bulk of the body is made up of muscle.

Knowing something about the basic anatomy and physiology will help koi-keepers better understand their fish's requirements to survive and thrive.

Body shape and size

The basic shape of a koi can be described as "fusiform," which means a thick trunk tapering forward and backward to a narrower head and tail. The body shape of contemporary koi differs from that of its ancestors because it has been manipulated through selective breeding to satisfy our preferences.

Viewed from above, the ideal shape is torpedo-like, with the widest part just behind the gills. Viewed in profile, the body should have its highest part just in front of the dorsal fin and the head must be nicely rounded, never square or pinched. The ideal height-to-length ratio is between 1:2.5 and 1:3.

A rounded rather than oval girth is desirable. Oval girths make the koi appear slender, and slender koi often swim with ungraceful, whip-like movements. The part of the body between the end of the dorsal fin and the caudal fin is known as a peduncle, and a thick peduncle adds to a positive first impression of a koi.

A koi's length is taken to be the distance from the nose to the tip of the tail fin. The height is measured from the abdomen at the base of the ventral fin to the start of he dorsal fin on the dorsal ridge.

Females have a fuller and bigger body, which is much preferred over the usually smaller and more slender male body. During the first two years of life, males grow faster than females but after this, a female koi can quickly surpass a male in length and girth.

AVERAGE WEIGHT AND LENGTH BY AGE		
AGE (years)	LENGTH (cm/in)	WEIGHT (g/oz)
<1	6 (15) 7 (18) 8 (20) 10 (25)	2 (60) 4 (120) 7 (210) 12 (350)
1–2	12 (30) 16 (40)	20 (550) 40 (110)
2–3	20 (50) 24 (60)	80 (2,200) 160 (4,500)
3–5	28 (70)	390 (11,000)

LATERAL VIEW OF A KOI

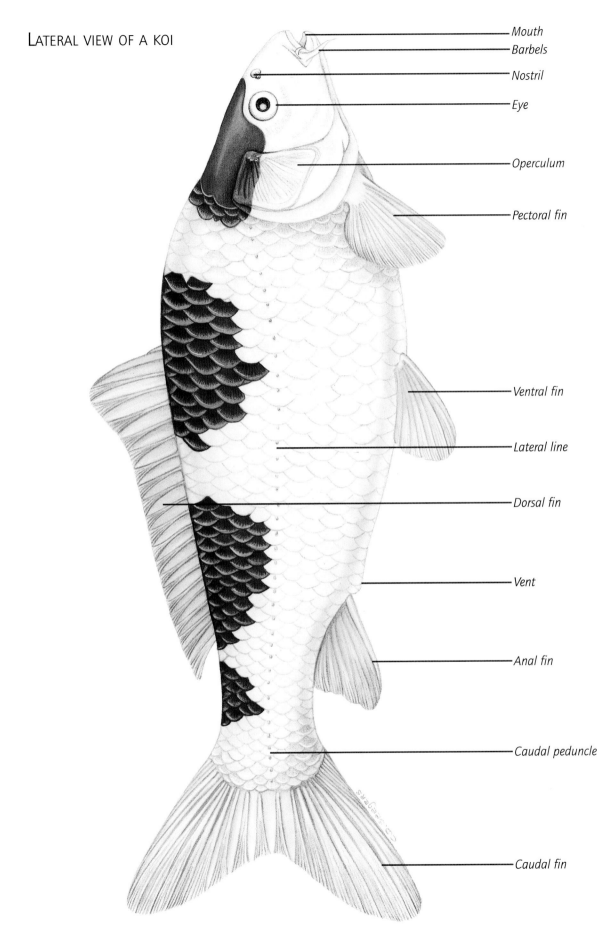

Mouth

Barbels

Nostril

Eye

Operculum

Pectoral fin

Ventral fin

Lateral line

Dorsal fin

Vent

Anal fin

Caudal peduncle

Caudal fin

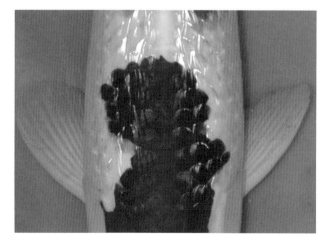

Fins

Koi have three single fins: the dorsal fin, on the back, is the principal stabilizing fin; the tail, or caudal, fin is the main source of propulsion; while the anal fin acts like a small keel, helping to stabilize movement.

There are two sets of paired fins. The pectoral fins are used to brake, back-paddle, and execute rapid turns while the ventral or pelvic fins are used for horizontal and vertical movement. Only the pectoral fins are connected to the skeleton.

A fin is made up of layers of specialized skin with fin rays as a supportive structure. The fins are scaleless with little blood supply and hence prone to injuries and disease, such as split fins, fin rot, and tail rot. Fins have the remarkable ability to regenerate and can quickly heal.

Scales

The scale is a bony plate covered by a layer of epidermis with its base in the dermis. Scales are thin and round with a smooth surface and a clear pattern of radiating lines crossed by concentric circles, which reveal the fish's growth periods. The whole scale is covered by an epithelium that has mucus-secreting glands.

Together, the mucus layer, scales, and skin form the first line of defense against injury and infection. If disease, parasites, infectious bacteria, or injuries breach this protective barrier, they can upset the osmotic balance, and create opportunities for pathogens to invade. Lost scales will regenerate, although they might be slightly different in shape and hue.

The scales are arranged in rows across the width of the body. A fish with a normal appearance of scales is called *wagoi*. *Doitsu* varieties have completely different scalation. Depending on the arrangement of the scales, the fish could be *kawa-goi* (leather carp), with no scales at all or only a few on each side of the dorsal fin; or *kagami-goi* (mirror carp), with a continuous row of scales from the neck to the anterior point of the dorsal fin, separating into a row of scales either side of the dorsal fin and continuing to just before the tail fin. In addition, there is a row of scales along the lateral lines. *Doitsu* koi with only a scattering of scales are known as *ara-doitsu*.

Top *Close-up of a pectoral fin with pigmentation.*
Center *Close-up of a scale, showing color variation.*
Bottom Ginrin *scalation appears iridescent or sparkling due to deposits of guanine crystals in the scales.*

Skin

Unlike land-based animals, which have a skin as their outer protective covering, fish have a cuticle. This is a double structure, made up of an external epidermis and an internal dermis, within which are situated nerves, blood vessels, pigment cells, and scales.

There are four types of color pigment cells, collectively known as chromatophores: melanophore (containing tyrosine and phenols for black pigment), xanthophore (with yellow carotenoid pigment), erythrophore (with red carotenoids), and leucophores (with guanine for white pigment). Combinations of pigment cells provide all the colors of koi, such as red and yellow combining to create orange, or black and yellow mixing to become brown.

The number of pigment cells is fixed from birth, and the amount of color will not increase with age. However, the color will develop (emerge, intensify, and gain sheen) if the chromatophores are deep-lying. Chromatophores on the surface of the skin result in thin and fading colors.

Pigment cells occur in both the scales and skin. In the scales they could occur either within a scale or on the underside of the scales. They could lie within the skin or just below the skin. Pigment cells mature with age, some taking a long time to become established. Black sometimes remains submerged for many years, only being revealed as gray or blue smudges. Red pigment cells often appear orange-red in young koi, maturing into a cinnamon red.

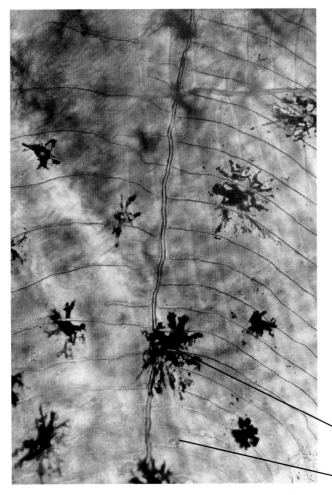

Pigment is determined by genetics and, while color can be enhanced, it cannot be created.

Expanded black pigment cell.

Yellow carotenoid pigment cell.

A microscopic image of black and yellow pigmentation in the skin, which together form a brown appearance overall.

Black color markings sometimes seem to shift from one place to another—a phenomenon called "wandering sumi"— but this is actually just one group of pigment cells submerging deeper and another group emerging. Pigment cells expand and contract as they mature. They also respond to nerve and hormonal signals that enable changes to be made to both color and intensity in the short and long term.

Koi are sensitive to strong light, which is why fish that show shiny black patterns in their pond environment can appear faded when displayed in bright sunlight at a koi show. This type of black color is known as *nabe-sumi*.

In addition to pigment cells there are iridocytes, which can best be described as tiny reflective flat crystals within normal skin cells. Iridocytes have different reflective properties,

depending on where they are positioned in the skin. Those closest to the surface give the fish a silvery appearance (*fukurin*). In combination with chromatophores, the iridocytes produce reflective colors (*hikari*), such as gold, on the surface. They are also involved in creating a blue color, as a result of deep-lying black pigment with iridocytes in the mid-layers of the skin. Iridocytes interfere with the light to give a blue color. Iridocytes can also be present within scales where guanine crystals, in the form of plates, transform the iridocytes into "mirror cells," or what is known as *ginrin* scalation in koi.

Iridocytes are tiny reflective cells that give koi a shiny silver or gold reflection.

Cardiovascular system

The heart circulates blood through a system of arteries and veins. Blood passing through the gills is oxygenated before being sent on to the tissues.

As there is no division between oxygen-rich arterial blood and oxygen-depleted venous blood, the koi's "primitive" cardiovascular system makes these fish vulnerable to low oxygen saturation levels (see page 76).

Respiratory system

The respiratory system is made up of gills. The gill arches and the primary and secondary lamellae are supported by a system of capillaries and blood vessels, creating a large surface area where blood and water are in close contact. A countercurrent system, in which the blood is pumped in the opposite direction to the water flow, allows for gaseous exchange. The efficiency of the gas exchange is crucial because water carries only a low level of dissolved oxygen (see page 76).

Gill disease upsets the koi's osmotic balance. Osmosis is the movement of water and electrolytes across a semipermeable membrane between two solutions of different concentrations. In practice, this means that water will favor diffusion to the more concentrated side (the fish) while electrolytes will favor movement out of the fish.

Like all freshwater fish, a koi must constantly rid itself of excess water via the kidneys. At the same time, it needs to reclaim lost electrolytes, which it does via special cells in the gill membranes. By adding salt (electrolytes) to the water, the osmotic pressure difference can be lowered, reducing the stress on the fish's system.

The koi's metabolism results in a buildup in the blood of nitrogenous waste products such as ammonia and purine. Ammonia, which is extremely toxic, is excreted into the water by diffusion via the gills. Purine and other larger waste compounds are excreted via the kidneys as urine.

Above A healthy gill has a bright red color.
Top Close-up of the gill plate.

Digestive system

The koi's digestive system is not typical of fish. One salient difference is that the fifth gill arches are modified to feature gill rakers (*saiko*) but no gill filaments. They also house six pharyngeal teeth the fish uses to "chew" with by pressing food against padded plates at the base of the skull. Koi use the *saiko* to filter plankton and other food particles from the water.

Because they do not have a true stomach, just a gut with certain areas involved in different digestive functions, koi cannot store food and therefore feed virtually continuously. Their intestines are long and curled and solid waste is excreted via the anal pore. The digestive organs include a large hepatopancreas and gall bladder.

Koi are prone to obesity when overfed, and koi-keepers are sometimes guilty of not giving sufficient consideration to feeding their fish a balanced diet. Fat cells are deposited in the hepatopancreas to the detriment of the normal functioning of these organs. Chronic obesity is often ignored as a contributing factor in a koi's poor health and limited life span.

Senses

The eyes, barbels, nostrils, and lateral lines represent the sensory organs that enable koi to search for food efficiently, as well as respond rapidly in order to avoid enemies and threats.

A short upper pair and a longer lower pair of barbels at the mouth are equipped with chemical sensors to help find food.

Nostrils, situated above the barbels, lead to a cavity with sensory organs that assist with smelling food and pheromones (scent signals released in alarm or for sexual communication).

Sight is important for detecting surroundings, predators, and certain types of food. The koi's eyes are located on the sides of the head and move independently for monocular vision. The eyelids are not movable, but the eyes roll in their cases to a limited degree. It is known that koi can detect color.

Lateral lines run along both the sides of the koi's body, where they can be seen as a row of scales extending from the head to the tail. Fully scaled koi have 33 to 36 scales on each lateral line, each of which has an external pore leading to a channel filled with a viscous solution. Within this channel lie neuromast, or receptor, cells that transmit their messages via the lateral line nerve to the brain. The neuromast cells are chemical and tactile organs through which koi can interpret sensations. More of these pores are arranged in a horseshoe pattern on the parietal area of the head.

Balance and sound detection are achieved by means of the inner ears, which are connected to the swim bladder (see page 30) via the Weberian ossicles, a set of modified vertebrae that amplify low-frequency sounds.

The barbels can be clearly seen in this view of a koi.

The lateral line is a key sensory organ for koi.

ANATOMY OF A KOI

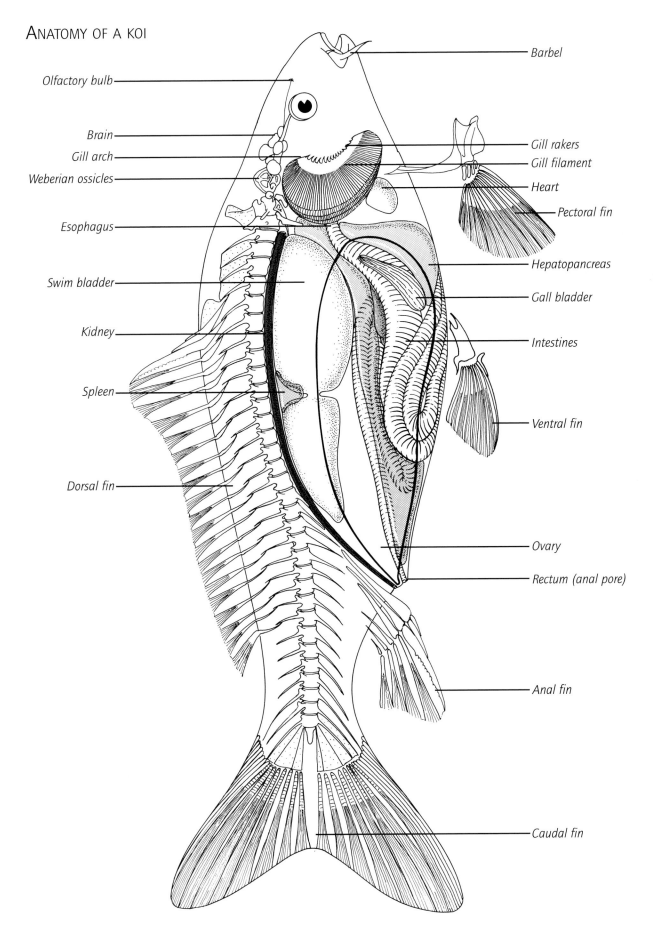

Olfactory bulb

Brain

Gill arch

Weberian ossicles

Esophagus

Swim bladder

Kidney

Spleen

Dorsal fin

Barbel

Gill rakers

Gill filament

Heart

Pectoral fin

Hepatopancreas

Gall bladder

Intestines

Ventral fin

Ovary

Rectum (anal pore)

Anal fin

Caudal fin

Nervous system

A koi's nervous system is made up of the brain, spinal cord, and peripheral nerves, which together collect and correlate stimuli that trigger the desired reactions by means of muscular movement, the release of endocrinal hormones and other body functions. The autonomic part of the nervous system controls vital functions such as the heartbeat, circulation, respiration, blood pressure, and so on.

Fish of the cyprinid family, including koi, are able to regulate their buoyancy by means of a swim bladder.

Reproductive system

Koi do not have external genitalia with which they can be sexed. Koi-keepers rely on body and fin shape to distinguish the sexes of their fish. Females have bigger, rounder bodies whereas males are usually smaller and more slender. During the spawning season, mature males develop tubercles on the head, body, and fins. These have a hard outer layer of keratin (similar to the substance of hair and nails on mammals) presumably to improve sexual contact between spawning fish.

The male testes produce milt (seminal fluid and sperm) and the female ovaries produce eggs that develop within the oviducts until they are released during spawning.

Urinary system

A long and irregular band of dark red tissue with two thin, flat "wings" constitute the paired kidney organs. The kidneys filter the blood for excessive water and metabolic wastes, which are excreted as urine via the urethra in the anal pore. They also play a vital role in regulating the concentration of electrolytes in the blood. Various structures within the kidneys contribute to the lymphatic and immune systems of the fish as well as secreting cortisol in reaction to a pituitary stress signal.

Swim bladder

The swim bladder is responsible for buoyancy and upright posture. It is an air-filled chamber with an interconnected front and rear section, situated in the upper part of the body cavity. Any disease that affects the swim bladder will cause the air in it to be lost and replaced with inflammatory fluid. This will affect the fish's buoyancy, causing it to sink to the bottom.

Life span

Koi-keepers in Western countries are not accustomed to very old koi, partly because the hobby is still relatively new in the West and partly because of the lack of knowledge and skill needed to nurture the fish into long life. In Japan, the life expectancy of koi is around 40 years. In the West, however, the average koi seldom lives beyond 15 years of age. One reason for the lower life expectancy might be the quest to create fish with "perfect" body shapes, which can go hand in hand with providing an over-rich diet, resulting in obesity and liver failure.

Under ideal conditions, however, koi can grow very old. In koi lore there is a persistent anecdotal account of a *Higoi* named Hanako that lived to a ripe old age of 228 years (some versions say 227 years). Her long life may be attributed to the fact that she was kept in a pond in a mountainous region subject to long, cold winters. When she died she was 30 inches (77 cm) long and weighed 20 pounds (9 kg). Despite the claims, Hanako's age was never scientifically proven.

Habitat

Koi do not occur naturally in the wild. While they can survive if they have accidentally escaped or were deliberately released, their coloration makes them easy prey. Because they are deliberately cultivated to be kept as a fish collection, their "natural" habitat can be considered to be a concrete pond.

In Asia, it is common practice to move koi from concrete ponds to earth dams (also called mud ponds) in spring and summer. Here the fish can revert to their natural state, foraging for food continuously for 20 hours a day. In this low-stress environment, and with good-quality water, significant growth is possible. Compared with a one-year-old koi reared in a concrete pond, a similar fish kept in a natural dam or pond for a two-year period will outstrip the other by as much as 12 inches (30 cm).

At the beginning of winter, the fish are usually taken out of the earth dams in order to prepare them for shows.

In Japan, koi are moved to earth dams during the summer. This allows them to forage for food naturally, and gain more weight and strength than their concrete pond equivalents.

Koi varieties

Koi-keepers refer to 15 varieties, or groupings, as defined by Zen Nippon Airinkai (ZNA), the Japan-based international promoter of koi-keeping, which sets standards for the appreciation and showing of koi.

The most definitive guidelines were published by the late Dr. Takeo Kuroki (former honorary chairman of the ZNA) and Reinosuke Nogami (chief of the ZNA's Appreciation Bureau) in a series of articles in *Nichirin* magazine in 1997 and 1998. Much of this chapter is based on their views.

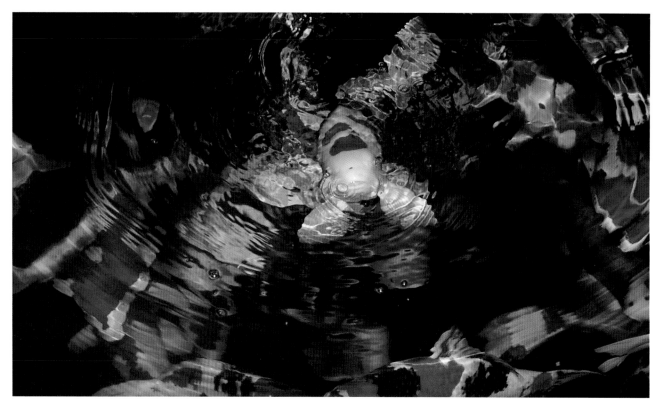

Throughout the world, koi-keepers acknowledge the official groupings as established by the ZNA, the international authority on koi, although many keepers have personal preferences regarding their favorite variety.

A recognized koi group can consist of a single variety (such as *Kohaku*), a grouping of related color variations (*Utsurimono*, for example), or even a group of totally unrelated or partially related varieties and their variations (such as *Kawarimono*).

Many pattern types are found in both the single varieties and the many variations within them. Variations often have commonly used descriptive names. *Inazuma Kohaku*, for example, is a pattern variation of *Kohaku*.

Koi appreciation differs from one country to the next, and can be influenced by fads or personal preference (both of which have a habit of changing). However, when it comes to appreciating the intrinsic quality of koi, it is body shape that takes precedence, and koi-keepers need to understand how body shape develops over time and how different varieties find expression in different body and bone structures.

Each variety has its preferred pattern placements, which serve as guidelines rather than absolutes. The beauty of a pattern is in its balanced uniqueness, but there can never be any compromising on body shape, skin quality, and grace.

"Ground" refers to the body or background color; markings are small or large groups of colored scales; and the pattern is the combination of the markings on their own and in conjunction with the ground color. Basic Japanese terminology is used for describing features (see Glossary, pages 150–53).

Throughout this chapter, the photographs include examples ranging from young to adult koi, to show the often dramatic development in body, color, and pattern they can undergo as they mature.

It happens with great frequency that a young koi-keeper will enter a dealer's shop, point out a photograph in a book or magazine and say: "I want one like that." Fish in photographs are usually prize winners and, even if they were readily available, it is doubtful whether an enthusiastic koi-keeper would be willing to part with most of his or her life savings to obtain one! Perhaps this chapter will educate koi-keepers to say instead: "I want a fish that could develop into one like that."

Fifteen variety groups

Kohaku Red markings on a white ground.

Sanke Red and black markings on a white ground.

Showa Heavy black markings on the head and body to complement the red markings, all on a white ground.

Bekko A "stepping stone" pattern of black markings on a white, red, or yellow ground.

Utsurimono White, red, or yellow ground on which a bold, often continuous, *sumi* pattern is laid.

Asagi Light or dark blue ground with red markings on the jaw and abdomen.

Shusui The *doitsu* (scaleless) version of the *Asagi*.

Koromo Scales "robed" (outlined) in blue or black to create a mesh pattern on the red markings of *Kohaku*, *Sanke*, or *Showa*.

Goshiki Five-colored koi with light or dark blue ground; the ground scales are robed in blue.

Kawarimono All nonmetallic koi, or any varieties not conforming to the standards of the other varieties, including single-colored koi.

Hikari-Mujimono Single metallic colors and their *matsuba* and *ginrin* variations.

Hikari-Moyomono All metallic koi with patterns of two or more colors (other than those bred out of *Utsuri* types).

Hikari-Utsurimono Metallic versions of *Showa* and *Utsurimono*.

Tancho Koi of any variety or subvariety that display a single circular red marking on the head. (For judging purposes, only *Kohaku*, *Sanke*, and *Showa* are grouped into *Tancho*.)

Kinginrin Koi of any variety that display shiny scales along the flanks or length of the back.

Definitions of terms

hi red, as a color, marking, or pattern

sumi black, as a color, marking, or pattern

shiro white, as a color

tobi-hi a small *hi* marking isolated from the main pattern

doitsu koi without scales

wagoi koi with normal scales

ground base color of the scales

mono thing or object

moyo pattern or design

moyomono patterned thing

bu the size grouping at a koi show

muji plain

(For detailed explanations and definitions of other terms refer to the Glossary, pages 150–53.)

Among the 15 groups, *Kawarimono* is the biggest overall, as it comprises several distinct varieties and variations (that at first seem totally unrelated).

None of the varieties should be considered superior to the others, although some koi-keepers maintain that *Gosanke* (the collective name for *Kohaku*, *Sanke*, and *Showa*) are the only worthwhile koi. Each variety has its own specific charm and its own challenges.

Kohaku

There is a saying that "the road to *Nishikigoi* begins and ends with *Kohaku*." This can be interpreted in a number of ways: first, that although most enthusiasts purchase *Kohaku* as their first koi, they soon abandon them because of the difficulties in getting specimens that will retain their quality over many years. However, as koi-keepers' pond and collection-management skills improve, they gain the courage to introduce *Kohaku* again. Second, koi-keepers soon become enchanted with the sometimes subtle, sometimes bold features of other varieties, before eventually returning to the dignified beauty of *Kohaku*. A third interpretation is that *Kohaku* is the prototype of modern koi varieties and therefore the king of them all. Proof of this may lie in the fact that *Kohaku* dominate in the winning lineups at koi shows.

Color

Kohaku have red markings (*hi*) on a white ground. Without a strong white ground, the *hi* pattern will show up as inferior, irrespective of the quality of the *hi*. The *hi* needs to be contrasted with white to show it to its full advantage. The ideal white ground is clear, unclouded, fine-textured, and even, with a soft, sheer look. It is difficult to get the same quality of white extending from the tip of the nose to the tail, and many *Kohaku* show an unattractive yellowish nose.

The *hi* should be a fine, uniform red color and have thickness (depth) to it. There are two kinds of *hi* color. One has a purple hue, with color that appears thick and does not fade easily, but lacks refinement.

The preferred *hi* has an orange hue, which is difficult to establish and can fade quickly. However, when this *hi* does become established, it appears bright and soft, and looks graceful and refined. In some *Kohaku*, a palish *hi* develops

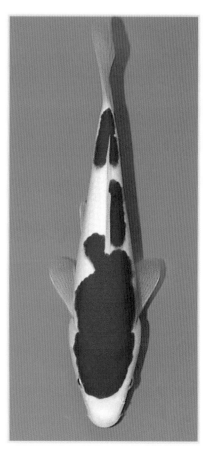

Kohaku, *18 inches (20 cm)*.

Kohaku, *10 inches (25 cm)*.

Kohaku, *22 inches (55 cm)*.

with age outside of the *hi* markings. This secondary development of *hi* (*nibban-hi*) is usually not big or distinct enough to form a marking, but it is a distracting feature and may indicate poor-quality breeding.

In a state of finish, the *hi* markings do not show up as individual scales but appear as a smooth carpet of color. Within a *hi* marking, an individual scale that is pale or has lost all color (*kokesuki*) is a defect. What is tolerated is the white ground breaking through the *hi* marking as a distinctive window (*mado-aki*).

A blemish on the white, such as a black spot (*goma, shimmie*) that is usually smaller than a single scale, or a small *hi* marking that is isolated from the main pattern (*tobi-hi*), is considered a flaw.

Markings and patterns

The distribution of *hi* markings should not be sparse or lopsided because it would make the *Kohaku* look impoverished in color and pattern. A *Kohaku* with no *hi* marking on the head is called *boze*. If the fish has a strong *hi* pattern on the front part of the body extending to the head, it is *bongiri*. Neither *boze* nor *bongiri* has any esthetic value. The same applies to *Shiro-Bo* (white all over with no trace of *hi*), *Aka-Bo* (red all over with no trace of white), and *Aka-Hajiro* (red body with white pectoral fins). *Aka-Hajiro* competes in the *Kawarimono* variety grouping, where it does have merit.

Kohaku, *34 inches (85 cm).*

Kohaku, *34 inches (85 cm).*

Head markings (*hachi*)

The preferred *hachi* is eye-catching, neat, and positioned above the line of the nose but no further back than the line of the eyes. If the marking is more or less round and separated from the rest of the *hi* pattern, it is known as *maruten*. Odd-shaped head markings are named *katsubera* (shoehorn). A *kuchibeni*, a small lipstick-like mark on the upper lip, is popular.

Several types of head markings are not tolerated and some are deemed undesirable. However, any other superior qualities should be the redeeming factor for anything undesirable. If the entire head is covered in *hi* it is called *menkabure* (this vestige of the *Kohaku*'s original ancestors is not tolerated). When the marking continues down to the mouth, it is described as *hanatsuki* (*tsukidashi*). *Mekazura* refers to a marking that covers the eyes or appears on the chin. A *hi* marking on the gill plate is a *hoaka*. None of these hold great appeal.

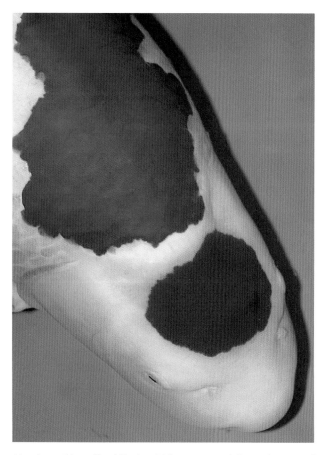

Head markings (hachi) *should be separated from the rest of the* hi *pattern, as seen on this* maruten Kohaku.

Body markings

The pattern should be strong, stable, and symmetrical to create the impression of balance and gracefulness. There are two distinct types of markings; bigger markings are known as *omoyo* and smaller ones as *komoyo*. Markings must appear along the entire length of the body and wrap down to below the lateral line.

Inexperienced koi-keepers tend to favor young *Kohaku* with defined patterns of smaller markings. However, as the *Kohaku* grows the pattern will become underemphasized. Experienced koi-keepers will recognize a young *Kohaku* with a big, but still dynamic, pattern and understand that because a koi's growth happens from the belly region upward, the bigger pattern on a small *Kohaku* will, with growth, separate into nicely sized, well-positioned markings.

Ippon-hi (also called *moyo*) is a continuous, unvaried marking reaching from the head to the base of the tail. The pattern has no accents and a monotonous appearance, unlike the much-prized *inazuma* pattern that is staggered across the length of the body like a thick bolt of lightning.

Danmoyo, a stepped pattern, is favored. Markings arranged in two groups are called *Nidan Kohaku*; three groups are *Sandan Kohaku*; four groups are *Yondan Kohaku*; and a pattern of five groups is *Godan Kohaku*.

Kura describes a marking that appears as a saddle across the back. If there are three saddles, the *Kohaku* will be known as *mitsu-kura*.

A *Kohaku* should not have patterning on only one side of the body (*kata-moyo*). Too few markings on the rear will make it appear "light in the rump" (*shiri ga karui*), while too many markings in this region make it "heavy in the rump" (*shiri ga omoi*). Nor should the pattern be so big as to show too little white, or too small, showing too much white.

The pattern should have a definite stop in the tail region. The scaled area just before the tail is called the *ozuke* and this is where the pattern should end. The furthest part of the rear marking is the *odome* (or *ojime*). An *odome* extending to the tail is considered to lack elegance. Ideally, markings should be distributed in a way that creates a balanced pattern.

Hi is generally not tolerated on the fins (although this is less of a fault now than in former days); the only exception is an extension to the base of the pectoral fin (*moto-hi*) of a marking that wraps deep down the body. Strong but small *moto-hi* is often seen in *Kohaku* show winners. Any *sumi* on the pectoral fins is sufficient reason to dismiss the fish as not a *Kohaku*.

Small spots of *hi* (*tobi-hi*), seldom covering an area of more than two scales, are often seen on the sides and abdomen of *Kohaku*. In bigger *Kohaku*, *tobi-hi* are not considered a major fault unless they spoil the overall appearance. *Tobi-hi* that appear near the *kiwa* of markings on the shoulder and middle part of the back are considered an eyesore.

The *kiwa* is the border between the posterior (back) edge of a marking and the white ground. Its quality depends on the clear cut of the *hi* marking on the scales. The most appreciated *kiwa* is where the *hi* stands out in bold relief on the edges of the scale (*honzome*, also called *maruzome*). The more defined the cut, the better the appearance of relief.

Sashi, the border between the anterior (front) edge of a marking and the white ground, shows up as a faint, blurred red, because the adjoining scales of the white ground overlap onto the first line of *hi* scales. This is considered to be a good indicator of the thickness of the pigmentation and hence of quality. *Sashi* is appreciated when it is evenly arranged over a half or full width of a scale. Irregular or unevenly arranged *sashi* is not attractive.

Variations

Apart from *wagoi* (normal-scaled) *Kohaku*, there are *doitsu* and *ginrin* variations. In competitions, *doitsu Kohaku* compete with normal-scaled *Kohaku* but *ginrin Kohaku* feature in the *Kinginrin* variety.

A *Kohaku* with only a single *hi* marking on the head falls under the *Tancho* variety. An appealing oddity among the *doitsu* is the "Napoleon *Kohaku*," which has a *hi* pattern on either side of the abdomen that resembles Napoleon's hat.

A less readily available variation is *Fuji-Kohaku*, which has silver-white lumps (*fuji*) on the head that disappear after two years of age. *Gotenzakura* has *hi* markings appearing as small clusters of red scales or "cherry blossoms" arranged symmetrically along the back. The metallic version of this is the *kin-zakura* with golden edges to the dappled red scales. *Kanoko-Kohaku* show a fawn-like pattern of dappled *hi* scales on a ground of white. Both the *Gotenzakura* and the *Kanoko-Kohaku* fall under the *Kawarimono* variety grouping.

Odome (ojime) *is the farthest part of the rear marking, before the tail.*

Sashi *is the border between the front edge of a marking and the white ground.*

Kiwa *is the border between the back edge of a marking and the white ground.*

When describing koi, certain terms can be used to indicate where body markings occur, or what they are.

Sanke

Sanke are tricolor koi with *hi* and *sumi* markings distributed across the body. *Sanke* is not merely a *Kohaku* with the addition of *sumi*; it is a koi with a perfect blend of *hi* and *sumi* markings on a ground of white.

The first consideration in appreciating *Sanke* is the white ground and an evaluation of the *hi*. The quality and patterning of the *sumi*, though of crucial value, is taken into account last. Apart from the balance of color, the white, *hi*, and *sumi* have to be of exemplary quality, something that is not easy to find. An old adage regarding the patterning of a *Sanke* that says if you eliminate the *sumi*, then a *Sanke* must be a good *Kohaku*, but if you then remove the *hi*, the fish must be a good *Bekko*.

Color and pattern

Ground   White ground must be revealed around the mouth and at the tail joint. It has to be near translucent with no muddiness, in order to juxtapose the *hi* and *sumi*.

Hi   The *hi* has to be of a uniform hue and lie deep. The same criteria as would apply to the *Kohaku* are relevant for the *Sanke*. The *hi* pattern should be in proportion to the white, as with *Kohaku*. A small *hi* pattern that would appear desolate on a *Kohaku* could be striking on a *Sanke* because of the addition of *sumi*. *Ippon-hi* appears monotonous on *Kohaku* but the same on *Sanke* could be impressive. Large, varied *hi* patterns hold more appeal.

Sumi   *Sumi* must always be clearly defined, with a balanced pattern and no distracting smudging. Because of its relation to the *hi* and white, *sumi* must conform to stringent criteria before it can be considered good and desirable. The *sumi* must be thick, uniform in color, and with a well-defined form complemented by sharp *kiwa*. It must have permanence and not deteriorate and scatter (*jari-zumi*, *bara-zumi*). The best quality *sumi*, described as *urushi-zumi*, has all the aforementioned qualities plus the bonus of a lacquer gloss.

Sumi can be like islands on white ground (*tsubo-zumi*), preferably close to *hi* markings, or overlapping the *hi* (*kasane-zumi*). *Tsubo-zumi* holds the greater appeal but a *Sanke* with large, good quality *kasane-zumi* can easily match this. A *Sanke* will frequently feature both types of *sumi* markings but, irrespective of the type, the *sumi* must not be blurred or appear sunken. A *Sanke* with *hi* and *sumi* markings that do not overlap at all, but alternate in a well-balanced arrangement, is called *Hanabatake Sanshoku*.

The *sumi* pattern should have a focal point (*miseba*). The most desired style is a *Sanke* with a bold *tsubo-zumi* marking on one of the shoulders (*kata-zumi*) and the rest of the *sumi* markings arranged in an appealing pattern across the length of the back to the *odome*. No *sumi* is tolerated on the head. A pattern with many small markings looks impoverished.

In young *Sanke*, the *sumi* markings often flow into one another like rather messy inkblots, but with age they should separate and gain definition.

Sanke have a tendency for *sumi* to appear more readily in the posterior; many koi show a clutter of *sumi* markings in the tail area, although a tail region devoid of *sumi* markings is far more elegant. Smallish, isolated patches of *sumi* (*hoshi*) and still smaller *sumi* markings (*goma*, *sesame*) are disliked.

Sanke may feature stripes on the fins. On the pectoral fins, these appear as two or three lines, called *tejima*, extending from the base but not quite reaching the tips. *Sumi* on the pectoral fins, such as the *motoguro* on *Showa*, is not favored. Strongly defined *tejima* indicate the stability of a *Sanke*'s *sumi*. Too many *sumi* stripes on the pectoral and tail fins (*ojima*) can spoil the value of a *Sanke* while the presence of *hi* in any of the fins is undesirable.

The *Sanke*'s *sumi* can easily be influenced by the quality of its environment and it could take up to five years to stabilize.

Sanke, *8 inches (20 cm)*.

Sanke, *16 inches (40 cm)*.

Sanke, *34 inches (85 cm)*.

Several *Sanke* bloodlines have been established with specific *sumi* characteristics:

Torazo The *sumi* is solid, stable, elongated in shape and most often displayed on a ground of persimmon *hi* on a near-transparent white skin.

Jinbei Purplish *sumi* of especially high luster, tending to be bigger and often appearing to link up with one another to form patterns. The *hi* is slightly purplish and the white is very fair.

Sadazo Small, well-defined *sumi* that do not overlap onto the prominent *hi* pattern.

Kichinai Smallish, jet black *sumi* arranged in triangular or wave-like patterns on the white ground. The *hi* pattern is stepped.

Matsunosuke Roundish, jet black *sumi* largely restricted to the white ground. The *hi* is intense and the white ground has a unique *fukurin*.

Variations

Aka-Sanke has *hi* that wraps the length of the body but leaves the nose and the belly white with smallish *sumi* markings layered onto the *hi*.

In addition to the normally scaled *wagoi Sanke*, this variety will also have *doitsu* and *ginrin*. Good *doitsu Sanke* are considered most attractive but their *hi* and *sumi* have a tendency toward instability and fading as they age.

The metallic variation of *Sanke* (*Yamatonishiki*) falls under the *Hikari-Moyomono* grouping; other scale variations, such as *Kanoko-Sanke* and *Tsubaki Sanke* (the latter has an entirely red body with *sumi* markings) are grouped under *Kawarimono*. The *Koromo Sanke* is grouped with *Koromo*, and *Tancho Sanke* is grouped under *Tancho*.

Showa

The second of the tricolor koi varieties is the *Showa*, which has a prominent *sumi* marking on the head, a *sumi* pattern with regularly linked markings and, often, an abundance of *sumi* in the fins (*motoguro*). Whereas the white, *hi*, and *sumi* on *Sanke* combine to create an impression of fresh, clear-cut looks, in *Showa* the combination results in complex, richly variegated patterns.

Showa patterns have changed over the years. In the older, more traditional style, up to 80 percent of the body was covered in *sumi* and *hi*, with the *sumi* pattern rising upwards from the abdomen, creating the impression of a black fish with red and white markings. The modern style, *Kindai Showa*, reveals substantially more white, to the point where the fish is often described as having a white ground.

Of all the varieties of koi, the *Showa* is the most susceptible to a faulty head and body shape. Heads often show up as flat, concave, and asymmetrical. No matter how imposing the quality of the colors or how striking the pattern, the *Showa* will have no show value if the head is deformed.

There are merits and demerits in a predominance of either white, *hi*, or *sumi* on a *Showa*. Personal preferences and fashion trends also dictate what is and is not acceptable.

Color

White This must have the same pure clarity as that of *Kohaku* and *Sanke*.

Hi The original *Showa* was bred out of *Ki-Utsuri* and *Kohaku* and the resulting *hi* was a yellow-red hue, but in the 1960s the quality of the *hi* was improved and brightened by breeding *Kohaku* to *Showa*. Nowadays both types of *hi* are seen but it is the brighter *Kohaku*-like *hi* that is preferred.

As in *Kohaku* and *Sanke*, the *hi* must be uniform, dense, and clear. The *kiwa* of the *hi* markings is seldom good. *Hi* markings must not be marred by *jari-zumi* or pale smears of *sumi*.

Sumi Clean, well-defined *sumi* must have an ebony-like luster and lie deep and thick. Because of the greater extent of *sumi* in *Showa*, it is almost impossible to have perfectly uniform quality. In places the *kiwa* of the *sumi* might be weak, but it should not be confused with submerged *sumi* (*shizumi-zumi*) that rises to the surface as the fish matures. Similarly, *shizumi-zumi* should not be confused with unstable *sumi* that will readily fade.

The *sumi* of a *Showa* could have originated in either *Tetsu-Magoi* (early examples) or *Asagi* (later examples). The indigo *Asagi sumi*, which does not rise from the abdomen but emerges just below the lateral line and upward, is more desirable although it takes many years to grow from thin gray to shiny, thick ink black. The *sumi* of the *Tetsu-Magoi* is a matte iron-blue known as *nabe-zumi* (charred-pan color) or *doro-zumi* (mud color). It rises from the abdomen in an attractive pattern but rarely gains a complete finish or sheen and appears without depth and dull.

It is difficult to determine the quality of *sumi* in a very young *Showa* as the *sumi* markings won't yet show depth and density. A well-known *Showa* breeder in Taiwan advises buyers to seek clues for good *sumi* by selecting young koi with bold *motoguro*; if the breeder or dealer permit handling, look for traces of dark *sumi* in the fish's mouth.

Pattern

Head The *sumi* marking on the head is a principal feature of the *Showa*. There are two basic patterns. The first is the *menware* (*hachiware*), typical of the older style, in which *sumi* starts at the nose and zigzags diagonally across the *hi* marking on the head to join up with the *sumi* marking on the shoulder. The other pattern is where a *hi* marking on the head lies between the *sumi* marking on the nose (*hana-zumi*) and another *sumi* marking on the shoulder, in the form of a V. The *hana-zumi* is considered to be the standard. A reasonable amount of white on the head and cheeks will brighten the face of the *Showa*.

Showa, *8 inches (20 cm), with underlying* sumi.

Showa, *24 inches (60 cm), with* motoguro *and* menware.

Showa, *34 inches (85 cm), with* fukurin *on white ground.*

Body The pattern of bold markings must stretch the entire length of the body. The pattern is similar to *Kohaku* and *Sanke* but, because the *sumi* appears in much larger patches, the overall impression of the *hi* pattern will be very different. An asymmetrical *sumi* pattern creates a powerful but dignified appearance when contrasted with the *hi* markings and highlighted by the white ground.

Fins Whereas *Sanke* has a striped pattern (*tejima*) on the pectoral fin, *Showa* has *motoguro*, a bold, solid marking starting at the base of the fin and covering a third to a half of the surface. Symmetrical markings on the pectoral fins promote the appearance of balance. In young *Showa*, the *sumi* might cover the entire pectoral fin but with time this becomes defined as *motoguro*, spreading somewhat as the fish grows older.

Pattern types

Boke-Showa The *sumi* scales appear blurred, usually more gray or blue than black. To reveal the *boke*, the scales ought to emerge from markings of pure white for maximum effect.

Hi-Showa The *hi* is predominant as either a single, big marking stretching from nose to tail or a *hi* marking with a few, small intrusions of white.

Kindai Showa Shows substantially more white ground, smaller and fewer *sumi* markings, and smaller *hi* markings.

Apart from the *wagoi*, there are *doitsu* and *ginrin Showa*. Metallic versions (*Kin-Showa* or *Gin-Showa*) fall under the *Hikari-Utsurimono* grouping. Other scale variations, for example *kage* and *kanoko*, come under *Kawarimono*. *Tancho Showa* belongs to the *Tancho* grouping.

Bekko

The ground of *Bekko* may be white (*Shiro-Bekko*), red (*Aka-Bekko*), or yellow (*Ki-Bekko*) on which a distinctive set of *sumi* markings is arranged, very much like stepping stones in a Japanese-style garden. Like *Utsurimono*, *Bekko* is dependent upon the quality and pattern of the *sumi* for its beauty. *Shiro-Bekko* and *Aka-Bekko* are accidental products of *Sanke* breedings because breeders do not try to breed true *Bekko*.

Ki-Bekko, which do not come out of the *Sanke* line, are very rare. Previously called *Ki-Botan* or Yellow Peony, they are classified as *Bekko* and have to meet all the criteria of the variety.

Color and pattern

Because of the simplicity of the coloring and pattern, there are strict criteria for selecting quality in *Bekko*. The preferred qualities of the *sumi* of a *Sanke* apply to a great extent for a *Bekko*. As with *Sanke*, there should be no *sumi* markings on the head (although this is tolerated if it occurs without detracting from the overall impression). A bold *sumi* marking on the shoulder (*kata-zumi*) is essential and must be complemented by a pattern of well-defined markings arranged in a neat and elegant pattern across the back.

Viewed individually, the *sumi* markings must be strong, but the pattern created by the markings must nevertheless be elegant. The *sumi* must be thick and uniform, with good density and *kiwa*. The overall appearance must be of shiny lacquer.

Lines often appear on the fins of *Bekko*. Two or three lines of *tejima* that appear etched onto the pectoral fins, starting at the base and ending short of the tip, are attractive, but too many lines in the dorsal and tail fins can spoil the appearance. In *doitsu* versions, the absence of *wagoi* scales make the *kiwa* of the *sumi* appear even sharper.

Doitsu Shiro-Bekko, *8 inches (20 cm)*.

Shiro-Bekko, *20 inches (50 cm)*.

Shiro-Bekko, *32 inches (80 cm)*.

The very best specimens appear to have had their *sumi* sculpted onto the ground color. *Ginrin* scalation can add significantly to the appreciation of *Bekko*.

Color types

Shiro-Bekko As the beauty of the *Shiro-Bekko* lies in the monotone contrast between white and black, the quality of the white ground is essential. The head, cheeks, and mouth must be white; a koi with an amber or yellow cast on those parts will lose its esthetic value. At a koi show, not a single *hi* marking, however faint, is permitted on a *Shiro-Bekko*.

Aka-Bekko Red right to the tips of the fins and on the belly. There may be a little white on the fins.

Ki-Bekko A uniform yellow body.

Aka-Bekko, *16 inches (40 cm)*.

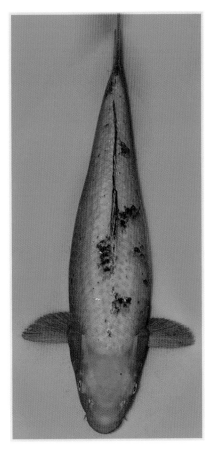

Ki-Bekko, *22 inches (55 cm)*.

Aka-Bekko, *28 inches (70 cm)*.

Utsurimono

An *Utsurimono* is an impressive koi with a white, red, or yellow ground onto which a bold, often continuous *sumi* pattern is laid. Black, red, and yellow markings, respectively, form *Shiro-Utsuri*, *Hi-Utsuri*, and *Ki-Utsuri*. The refined, elegant patterns give *Utsurimono* an appearance of majesty.

The *Utsurimono* was once considered to have a ground of the *sumi* of its ancestor *Asagi* lineage but the variety has undergone refinement to the point where the amount of white has been sufficiently increased to be considered as the ground color rather than pattern.

There are two interpretations of the Japanese word "*utsuri*." Traditionally it meant "reflections" and was used to describe how the *sumi* pattern was mirrored by the white, red, or yellow colors. "*Utsuri*" can also be interpreted as "to move or shift," referring to the way in which the *sumi* of the *Utsurimono* changes and shifts.

Many *Utsuri* originate from *Showa*, and the *Showa* lineage is sometimes revealed in the small, single-scaled *hi* markings (*tobi-hi*) that appear on the cheeks and belly of the *Shiro-Utsuri*. In warm water the *tobi-hi* are prominent, often fading completely in cool water only to re-emerge in the summer. If the *tobi-hi* cannot be seen when viewing the *Shiro-Utsuri* from above, it will not detract from the quality.

Color

Sumi The *sumi* is vital when appreciating the *Utsurimono* variety. Quality *sumi* has uniformity, good density with sharp *kiwa*, a high degree of gloss (*urushi-zumi*) and is not susceptible to change. Poor quality *sumi* is easy to spot; it appears matte and brownish (*nabe-zumi*), has unsatisfactory *kiwa*, tends to break up and scatter (*jari-zumi*), has often little or no gloss, and is easily affected by environmental changes or background colors that will cause it to blur and fade.

Where *sumi* meets white ground, submerged *sumi* shows as grayish blue through the skin, creating a beautiful feature rather than a fault.

The *sumi* ground takes time to establish itself as a pattern and in quality. "Wandering *sumi*" appears to shift from place to place as, depending on age and water conditions, the *sumi* rises to the surface or submerges. Koi-keepers may have to wait up to five years for the pattern to become fixed.

White To complement the *sumi*, the white ground must have depth, brightness, and no flaws; instead, the ground color must lift the *sumi* toward even greater boldness. An amber or yellowish tinge to the white, especially in the head region, spoils the appearance.

Pattern in the color types

Shiro-Utsuri In the older style of *Shiro-Utsuri*, the *sumi* pattern copies that of the *Showa* to create an impression of the *sumi* bursting open to reveal pure, vivid white patterning. Originally the *sumi* on the body would wrap deeply around from the back onto the abdomen, rising upward from there like mountain peaks (*maki-agari*). The modern style shows more white ground with a pattern of more delicate *sumi* markings. The older style appears imposing and dynamic whereas the new style is elegant and refined.

In *Shiro-Utsuri* the *sumi* pattern must spread along the length of the body. The *menware* head marking is typically a *sumi* marking on the mouth extending across the head into a bold shoulder marking (not necessarily in a continuous line). It is standard for *motoguro* to appear on the pectoral fins and this is considered a test of *sumi*'s quality. Definite, dark *motoguro* will reveal the strength of the *sumi*. A strong *sumi* presence can easily hide a physical deformity and, no matter how wonderful the *sumi* patterning, the *Shiro-Utsuri* has no esthetic value if it is deformed.

In some countries, a few isolated *hi* scales may be tolerated on the abdomen, provided they do not constitute a *hi* marking or spoil the overall appearance of the fish. No *hi* is tolerated on the pectoral fins, and specimens displaying this are not acknowledged as *Shiro-Utsuri*.

Hi-Utsuri This variation has a large amount of *hi* wrapping upward from the abdomen over the black ground color. The *hi* varies from light red to bright scarlet and must be uniform, reaching the extremities of the body. Colorless scales (koke-suki) in the hi will lower the value of the fish.

Its sumi pattern could be old or modern in style but must be eye-catching. The sumi of Hi-Utsuri tends to lack coherence and distracting jari-zumi will appear alongside sumi markings. Motoguro must be present.

Ki-Utsuri Hailing from the earliest days of Nishikigoi, at the beginning of the Meiji era, Ki-Utsuri was known as Kuro-ki Han (black with yellow pattern). The desirable yellow color must be bright, like autumn leaves. Like Hi-Utsuri, Ki-Utsuri tends to reveal jari-zumi. As it is difficult to attain a high gloss in both the yellow and the sumi as well as sharp kiwa, good specimens of Ki-Utsuri are rarely seen.

Other types

In addition to wagoi Utsurimono, this variety also features doitsu and other variations. In doitsu, the kiwa of the pattern appears much sharper and the contrast between the colors is strong and beautiful. Kin Ki-Utsuri falls under the Hikari-Utsurimono. Kage specimens with ground colors of white, yellow or red are grouped in Kawarimono. Ginrin versions fall under Kinginrin Group B.

Menware sumi divides the face or head in two, often in a Y-shape.

Shiro-Utsuri, 7 inches (18 cm).

Shiro-Utsuri, 20 inches (50 cm).

Hi-Utsuri, 30 inches (75 cm).

Asagi

The *Asagi-Magoi*, a mutation from wild carp (see page 13), was already known in the late 1880s, when it featured blue-black coloring and scales with a netting effect. Two branches come out of the *Asagi-Magoi*: the clear indigo *Konjo-Asagi* (an early ancestor of *Aka-Matsuba*, *Ki-Matsuba* and *Kigoi*), and *Narumi-Asagi* with scales having a dark indigo center and a paler surround. *Narumi-Asagi* gave rise to the modern day *Asagi* (and also to the varieties with a white ground: *Kohaku*, *Sanke*, *Shiro-Bekko*, *Goshiki*, *Aigoromo*, and *Shusui*).

Asagi have distinctive, simple, but austerely elegant qualities. Novice koi-keepers may consider them unassuming in appearance but experienced keepers admire the delicate scalation, blue coloring (*ai*), *hi*, and well-rounded body shape.

Color and pattern

Asagi have rows of precisely aligned, regular scales, called *kokenami*, each with a half-moon shape of clear, unclouded dark blue in the center, surrounded by paler blue. The scales create a mesh pattern with bright edges (*fukurin*). There are no scales on the head and the *Asagi* is completely bald.

The *ai* ranges from dark ultramarine to very pale blue and, irrespective of the shade, must appear bright, clear and uniform. The *ai* is complemented with *hi*, which is a bright, fiery red. *Hi* is present on the cheeks (*ago-hi*), often with white patches; to be impressive, the cheek markings must be symmetrical. On the body (*hara-hi*) the *hi* should preferably lie below the lateral line and not overlap the blue scales.

The pectoral and ventral fins also have *hi*, which should be restricted to the base of the pectoral fins (*Shusui-bire*). *Hi* on the mouth (*kuchibeni*) and the dorsal or tail fin will not distract from the *Asagi* if it has other outstanding qualities.

Asagi, *10 inches (25 cm).*   Asagi, *26 inches (65 cm).*   Hi-Asagi, *32 inches (80 cm).*

An interesting variation is the *Hi-Asagi* where the *hi* wraps from the belly upward to cover all of the back.

A darkening of the white head, *hi* rising onto the head and back, or *sumi* speckles (all usually associated with aging) will seriously decrease an *Asagi*'s esthetic value.

Because *Asagi* increase their *hi* year after year, koi-keepers should select young *Asagi* with a small *hi* pattern, confined to the lower abdomen. If the *hi* in a young *Asagi* is too dominant (rising high onto the flanks), it could indicate that the *hi* will spread beyond the desired limits, even turning the *Asagi* into an *Aka-Matsuba*. Avoid *hi* markings on the head that spread beyond the eye and toward the center of the head, and those along the cheek that create an ungainly "full beard."

Reject koi with scarring on the scales (which might never heal properly) or missing scales (which take a long time to regenerate and might not have the same shade of color).

Variations

There are five *Asagi* color types:

Konjo-Asagi Intense indigo-colored scales reaching to the edge of each scale.

Narumi-Asagi The "essential" *Asagi* has scales with a dark blue center and a pale blue surround.

Mizu-Asagi White-blue color, the palest of all the types and with no value whatsoever. Some have blurred *hi* markings on the side, earning them the nickname "*Okame*," which means "a moon-faced woman." (Also known as *Akebi-Asagi*.)

Asagi-Sanke Pale blue back, red head and flanks, and a pure white lower abdomen.

Taki-Asagi A white break separates the *hi* on the abdomen from the blue back. Sometimes described as the "Waterfall-*Asagi*" because the white pattern resembles a waterfall.

Sanke-Asagi and *Goshiki-Asagi* are hybrids of *Asagi* and are classified as part of the *Kawarimono*.

Good Asagi *scales have bright* fukurin *(edges), creating a clear mesh pattern.*

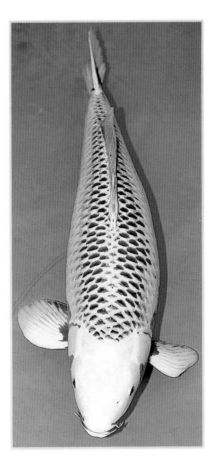

Konoko Asagi, *32 inches (80 cm).*

Shusui

This is the *doitsu* version of the *Asagi*. The characteristic feature of *Shusui* is a clear blue back, on which a line of large, dark blue scales are neatly arranged with a complementary *hi* pattern. Most points of appreciation for *Asagi* apply to *Shusui*.

Color and pattern

The blue ground should be reminiscent of an "autumn sky" in shades of ultramarine or royal blue. The bald head is a pale blue color. The blue ground must be of even quality and hue from the neck to the tail and from the dorsal line to just below the lateral line. The paler the blue, the more sharply it offsets the dorsal scalation and *hi* pattern. Neither the head nor back may have any spots or blurs.

The dark, large scales on the dorsal line are conspicuous and should therefore display neatly. The dorsal scalation should start as close as possible to the head and continue beyond the dorsal fin to reach the tail without being interrupted by crooked or absent scales. Black or gray scales will earn demerits. Single or clusters of superfluous scales (*muda-goke*) that appear between the lateral line and the dorsal arrangement will lower the value of the *Shusui*.

Shusui, *6 inches (15 cm)*.

Hana-Shusui, *14 inches (35 cm)*.

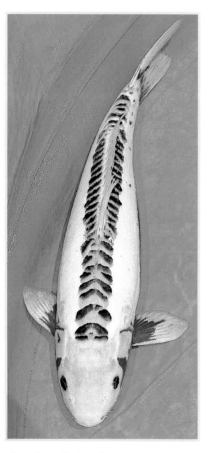
Shusui, *24 inches (60 cm)*.

The *hi* is the same fiery red as in *Asagi*. It should be confined to the chin, cheeks, and abdomen (except in *Hi-Shusui* and *Hana-Shusui*); with a symmetrical pattern on the cheeks and flanks. *Hi* also features prominently on the base of the pectoral fins (*Shusui-bire*), giving these koi a flamboyant look.

Variations

Four pattern types are acknowledged.

Hana-Shusui Apart from the *hi* pattern on the abdomen, a second line of *hi* runs between the lateral and the dorsal lines.

Hi-Shusui The red of the abdomen extends upward to cover all of the back.

Ki-Shusui A yellow *Shusui* with blue on the back.

Pearl-Shusui A *Shusui* with *fukurin* on the scales of the back.

Lesser-known variations are *Sanke-Shusui*, *Showa-Shusui*, and *Goshiki-Shusui*, all classified as *Kawarimono*, and *Ginsui* and *Kinsui*, which fall under *Hikari-Moyomono*.

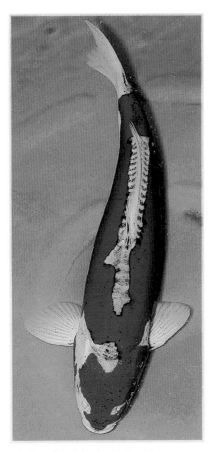

Hi-Shusui, *20 inches (50 cm).*

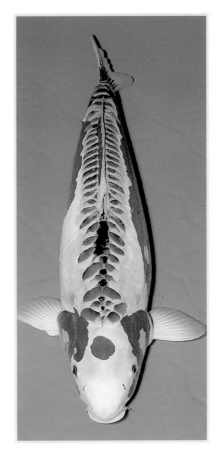

Shusui, *28 inches (70 cm).*

Koromo

Koromo is the Japanese term to describe the blue or black "robing" or outlining of scales on red markings that results in a mesh pattern. It also applies to the brushed or smeared effect of *sumi* onto *hi*. *Koromo* is the collective name for koi with *koromo* scalation.

Several distinctive *Koromo* types are acknowledged:

Aigoromo This is the most typical *Koromo* and is produced by breeding *Kohaku* to *Asagi*. For maximum effect, the *koromo* must be contrasted with a ground of thick but pure and unblemished white and the *hi* pattern must be as that of *Kohaku*. The addition of the *koromo* allows for a readily acceptable, more broken, and flowery pattern.

The robing for *Aigoromo* is blue *fukurin* (edging) in a half-moon shape on the posterior side of the scales. It should not extend onto the white ground but be confined within the *hi* marking. No robing should be seen on the head marking. *Moto-hi* but not *motoguro* is allowed on the pectoral fins.

It takes time for *koromo* to stabilize and mature. In most cases the robing will only achieve its full effect when a fish is four or five years old. A young fish with dirty-looking *hi* and just a hint of indigo will eventually achieve the desired quality of robing. Unfortunately, the white ground is prone to develop *jami*, or stains, making it is difficult to find outstanding specimens among large *Aigoromo*.

Budo-Goromo (*Budo-Sanke*) *Budo* can be translated as "grape" and the patterning must resemble clusters of grapes. The wine-colored markings are best revealed when they show up in relief on a top-quality white ground.

Koromo, *6 inches (15 cm).*

Koromo, *14 inches (35 cm).*

Koromo, *20 inches (50 cm).*

Sumi-Goromo As indicated by the name, the *koromo* will be *sumi* rather than *ai*. The *sumi* does not "fill" the scale but appears as though it was brushed on or smeared unevenly. It also does not have the *fukurin* effect as in *Aigoromo*. The *sumi* appears on the *hi* marking of the head and the overall impression of the koi is that it looks austere.

Koromo-Sanke A cross of *Aigoromo* and *Sanke*, it features a mesh pattern of indigo *koromo* over the *hi* markings of a *Sanke*. In other words, such a koi has two types of *sumi*, that of *Sanke* (*hon-zumi*) and of *Koromo* (*koromo-zumi*).

Koromo-Showa (*Ai-Showa*) A cross of *Aigoromo* and *Showa*. The indigo *koromo* creates a mesh pattern over the *hi* markings of a *Showa*. The impression is austere.

Aigoromo, *25 inches (63 cm)*.

Budo-Goromo, *30 inches (75 cm)*.

Sumi-Goromo, *26 inches (65 cm)*.

Goshiki

The *Goshiki* arose from breeding *Asagi* with *Sanke* to create a *Sanke* pattern overlaid on a blue ground. (*Goshiki* is pronounced *"gosh-ki,"* with the accent on the first syllable and the first "i" silent.) *"Go"* is the Japanese word for five and *Goshiki* is therefore a five-colored fish: white, red, black, light blue, and dark blue. The mixture of the colors reveals the white ground as purplish.

In 1995, *Goshiki* was promoted out of the *Kawarimono* group, where it had competed with many other subvarieties to become a variety in its own right.

Color and color types

Goshiki with a more pronounced *Asagi* patterning of dark blue robing of the scales on white ground, are considered to be in the modern style and are called *Kindai Goshiki* (also known as *Mameshibori-Goshiki*). Darker ground, the more classic style, is called *Kuro-Goshiki.*

Water temperature appears to affect the intensity of the ground. In cold water, a pale ground will turn dark, lightening again as the water warms.

Goshiki, *6 inches (15 cm).*

Kuro-Goshiki, *14 inches (35 cm).*

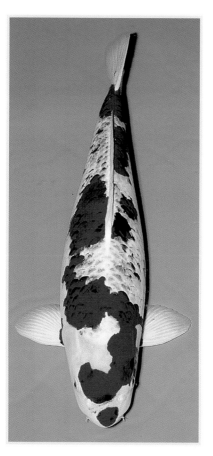

Kindai-Goshiki, *26 inches (65 cm).*

Pattern and pattern types

A typical *Kohaku* and *Sanke* pattern is preferred for the *hi* markings, which should not be too large or dominant because much of the appeal lies in the attractive ground.

The robing should be confined to the ground color, although some will appear on the *hi* markings. The head marking should be bold and clear, with bright *hi*. Small *hi* markings in the pectoral fins (*Goshiki-han*) can help create balance to the pattern. Streaks of *ai* or *hi* in the tail and dorsal fin are not ideal but can be tolerated.

Breeding *Goshiki* to *Sanke* and *Showa* produces *Goshiki-Sanke* and *Goshiki-Showa*. These are rare, making them true connoisseurs' fish. *Goshiki-Sanke* reveal big, bold *sumi* markings, on or overlapping the *hi* markings or on the ground color, while *Goshiki-Showa* have typical *Showa* markings and pattern. *Doitsu* and *ginrin Goshiki* are also found and can be very attractive.

Kuro-Goshiki, *22 inches (55 cm)*.

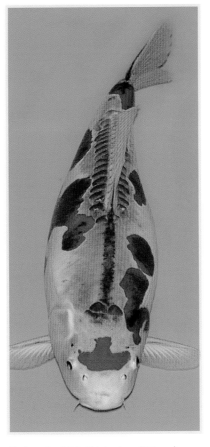

Doitsu-Goshiki, *34 inches (85 cm)*.

Goshiki-Sanke, *20 inches (50 cm)*.

Kawarimono

This is the biggest variety grouping in the traditional classification of koi. *Kawarimono* translates as "strange, different, odd" but it might be more apt to consider it as a group of unique variations of color, pattern, and scalation.

The varieties within *Kawarimono* are as fixed as any of the other groupings. Varieties such as *Karasugoi* and *Matsubagoi* can trace their lineages far back in koi history, while others emerged relatively recently. This grouping includes koi bred from crossing two varieties and which cannot be decisively included in the type of either parent.

Each of the member varieties has a definite status, despite being lumped together under the umbrella of *Kawarimono*.

As new varieties evolve, they will probably be added to *Kawarimono*. Those that gain widespread acceptance, as was the case with *Goshiki*, might one day be elevated into their own variety grouping.

Kawarimono can be daunting for the novice koi-keeper, who could find the many varieties too subtle. On the other hand, the *Kawarimono*'s refinement might be exactly what an experienced practitioner needs to add spice to a collection.

Karasugoi line

These are black koi with variations of white markings. The black must be as if the fish was dipped in black lacquer while the white parts must be clear. It must always appear majestic. ***Karasugoi*** *Karasu*, the Japanese word for raven, recalls the bird's glossy black feathers. The *Karasugoi* is black all over. The quality of the black is more intense than *Magoi*.

These koi hail from the *Konjo-Asagi* lineage. In the *doitsu* (scaleless) form, they can be very impressive and have high ornamental value.

Konoko-Kohaku, *31 inches (78 cm)*.

Kumonryu, *32 inches (80 cm)*.

Chagoi, *30 inches (75 cm)*.

Hajiro A black body with white revealed on the tips of the pectoral fins only. "*Hajiro*" means "white wings."

Hage-Shiro A black body with white tips to the pectoral fins and white on the nose, spreading over the head.

Yotsujiro A black body with a white head and white on the tail and pectoral fins.

Matsukawabake The white and black pattern changes with the seasons.

Kumonryu Also known as the "dragon fish" or "Moby Dick," this is the *doitsu* version of the *Karasu* lineages. It reveals more white than *Yotsujiro*. The white ground is revealed across the body and tends to expand in warmer water. Recent variations are *Beni-Kumonryu*, in which a large *hi* pattern has been introduced with astounding effect, and *Kikokuryu* and *Kinkiryu* with a more sparse golden yellow pattern.

Suminagashi (*Asagi-Suminagashi*) An *Asagi* pattern appears on the black, with each scale featuring a white border.

Matsubagoi line

The types reflect their *Asagi* inheritance. The scales have a black crescent shape, appearing in relief and arranged in a pattern that resembles a pine cone. *Aka-Matsuba* of exemplary quality are sought after by connoisseurs.

Aka-Matsuba *Matsuba* scalation on a ground of red.

Ki-Matsuba *Matsuba* scalation on a ground of yellow.

Shiro-Matsuba *Matsuba* scalation on a ground of white.

Matsuba-Doitsu The large scales on the back and along the lateral lines are *Matsuba* style.

Shusui line

A *doitsu* result from crossbreeding *Shusui* and *Sanke*, *Showa*, or *Goshiki*. In all cases the *sumi* must have exceptional depth and intensity, and the *sumi* markings must have good *kiwa*.

Sanke-Shusui Dark blue ground on the back, typical of *Shusui* with a *Sanke* pattern.

Hajiro, *30 inches (75 cm).*

Matsukawabake, *25 inches (63 cm).*

Yotsujiro, *16 inches (40 cm).*

Showa-Shusui Dark blue ground on the back, typical of *Shusui* with a *Showa* pattern.

Goshiki-Shusui Dark blue back, typical of *Shusui* with *Goshiki* coloring.

Kage

Kage means "shadow" and indicates an arrangement of scales, each with a black shadow, with the overall effect like that of a lattice overlaid on a white ground. In all instances the *sumi* must be clean, bright, and deep to reveal the *kage* to its full advantage. The white that borders the *kage* must be pure and intense to offset the scalation effect.

Shiro Kage-Utsuri and **Hi Kage-Utsuri** *Shiro-Utsuri* and *Hi-Utsuri* with white ground revealing *kage* scalation.

Kage-Showa *Showa* revealing *kage* scalation on white ground.

Plain-colored koi

Either solid brown, yellow, or blue-gray for which uniformity is demanded. These koi outgrow other varieties with ease. They are appreciated for their superb body shapes, size, and neat reticulation of the scales. Because of the simplicity of coloring and scalation, even a single scar will reduce the attractiveness of a plain-colored koi. *Kinginrin* variations are popular.

Chagoi Brown-yellow ground all over. The color is deeper along the scale edges, creating a faint mesh pattern. Young *Chagoi* tend to be olive-green, maturing into dark brown.

Kigoi Bright yellow all over. Some *Kigoi* have red eyes (*Akame-Kigoi*); such specimens are said to show a better skin tone and are prized collector's items. Faint scatterings of *hi* on the ground will lower the esthetic value.

Benigoi The *hi* is a vermillion red and covers the entire body.

Soragoi A gray-blue ground all over. The color is likened to the hue of "sky before the rain."

Ochibashigure, *6 inches (15cm)*.

Aka-Matsuba, *32 inches (80 cm)*.

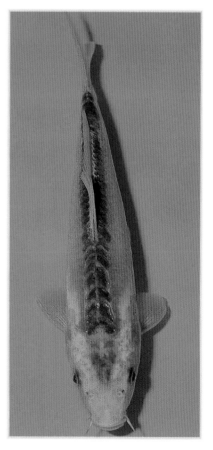
Midorigoi, *8 inches (20 cm)*.

Kanokogoi

Kanoko indicates a mottled pattern in which the *hi* scales do not combine to create large markings, but alternate with white scales to create a dappled effect. The effect is spoiled if the dappling is incomplete or patchy.

Kanoko-Kohaku Dappled *hi* scalation on a *Kohaku*.

Kanoko-Sanke Dappled *hi* scalation on a *Sanke*.

Kanoko-Showa Dappled *hi* scalation on a *Showa*.

Ochibashigure

Bred out of the *Chagoi*, this variation has an austere pattern of dark brown markings on a ground color that varies from light gray to green to brown. "Autumn leaves floating on water" is an excellent description of the overall impression. Each scale must appear to be individually embossed, and the pattern distinct with no blurring of the edges. Markings must be neither too small nor too bold and always elegant.

Aka-Muji and Aka-Hajiro

Aka-Muji Unstable or poor red, with the color covering the entire body and fins. Considered to be a low-quality variety, it is usually eliminated during culling. As it grows, it might lose all coloring and become a valueless *Shiro-Muji*.

Aka-Hajiro Bright red with the color covering the entire body and all fins except for the tips of the pectoral fins, which are white.

Other colors

The **Midorigoi** is a green-colored hybrid from *Shusui* and *Yamabuki-Ogon* origin.

Shiryu is a purple-colored koi. Though beautiful when young, the breeding of neither has been sufficiently fixed and they tend to get darker with age.

Sumi-Tancho, *7 inches (18 cm)*.

Beni-Kikokuryu, *22 inches (55 cm)*.

Leopard-Kumonryu, *6 inches (15 cm)*.

Hikari-Mujimono

Hikari is the Japanese word for "shining" and *Hikari-Mujimono* denotes single-colored koi with a metallic luster. The colors include gold, yellow, orange, red, and platinum. The group also includes *Kin-Matsuba* and *Gin-Matsuba*. These are some-times called "Leopard-*Ogon*" although *matsuba* is usually associated with the neat rows of tightly-packed, dark-centered pine cone-like scales. *Hikari-Mujimono* are very popular with koi-keepers because of their metallic luster and the quiet charm they introduce into a collection.

Color and color types

Because of the simplicity of the *Hikari-Mujimono* types, flaws or faults show prominently. Although they have no pattern, the scalation must be complete and perfectly aligned. It is essential that the *fukurin* shine with a uniform color, not only along the length of the back but also reaching down onto the abdomen. The metallic luster will quickly reveal any lost scales, healed injuries, or black smudges. The luster of the ground color must appear to radiate from within rather than be layered on the outside.

The head should be bright, without the slightest hint of a scar, blemish, or cloudiness, and its baldness must extend slightly onto the dorsal ridge. Deformities of the head regu-larly occur and such specimens must be avoided.

The pectoral fins must be of uniform shape and have a dis-tinct shine right to the tips. Koi in this group, especially the

Purachina, *10 inches (25 cm)*.

Yamabuki-Ogon, *21 inches (53 cm)*.

Orenji-Ogon, *28 inches (70 cm)*.

Ogon, have a tendency to grow too fat and develop a pot belly. The fish should be blessed with good length and girth.

Several color types have been established. The main one is the *Ogon*, the original golden (saffron) colored koi. A yellow-gold or lemon-gold variation bred from *Ogon* and *Kigoi* is known as *Yamabuki-Ogon*; the metallic deep-orange variation is *Orenji-Ogon* (Orange-*Ogon*). Platinum-*Ogon* (*Purachina*) is pure platinum-silver while those with mouse-gray silver are *Nezu-Ogon* (*Nezumi-Ogon*); if the mouse-gray is a particularly whitish color, it is known as *Shiro-Ogon*. The *Hi-Ogon* is a rare metallic red version. Peach-*Ogon* has found favor among Western koi hobbyists but is not as popular with connoisseurs.

The metallic *matsuba* variations were created by breeding *Ogon* with *Asagi*. Each scale has a black marking and the over-all effect is of a stylized pine cone on a lustrous golden ground, varying from pale to dark. *Kin-Matsuba* are only good if the scalation is perfectly arranged and the *fukurin* is exceptional. *Gin-Matsuba* has a platinum ground color.

Doitsu versions of the *Ogon*, Platinum-*Ogon*, and *Orenji-Ogon* are popular. A rarity is the *Mizuho-Ogon*, an orange-colored *doitsu Matsuba-Ogon* with shiny black *doitsu* scales on the back of the lustrous orange body.

For the purpose of koi shows, the *ginrin* versions of the *Ogon* varieties are grouped under *Hikari-Mujimono*.

Ghost koi are produced by crossing common carp with *Purachina* (Platinum-*Ogon*) or *Yamabuki-Ogon*. Ghost koi can be loosely defined as dark fish, with an incomplete silver or golden matallic skin and scalation, and with the body shape of a koi. A good quality Ghost may be those with a grayish-silver sheen and these are called *Nezu-Ogon* (*nezu* meaning gray and also the Japanese name for a mouse). Those of average quality that show a blackish body wih a silver or golden

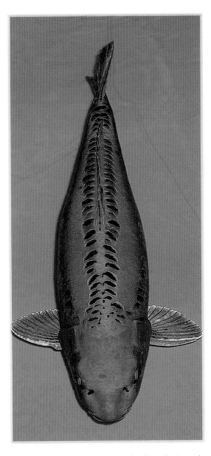

Doitsu Kin-Matsuba, *28 inches (70 cm).*

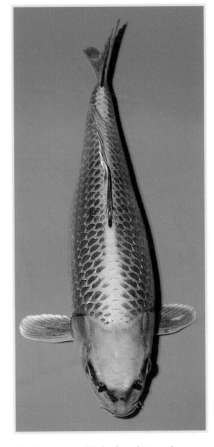

Kin-Matsuba, *22 inches (55 cm).*

Gin-Matsuba, *8 inches (20 cm).*

back are known as *Ginbo* and *Kinbo* respectively. The poorest quality are *Kin-Kabuto* and *Gin-Kabuto* with blackish bodies, a golden or silver pattern on the head and golden- or silver-edged scales.

Ghosts have become immensely popular, probably because they are easy and cheap to produce while not requiring strong selection skills, and because of their vigorous growth and strong constitution. The name and abnormal interest most likely stem from earlier koi publications pointing out the often-seen peculiar head markings that resemble a death skull on *Gin-Kabuto* and *Kin-Kabuto*.

Despite their popularity, the connoisseur sees these koi as valueless, because they represent a regression toward the common carp, rather than improved refinement.

Right Ginrin Ogon, *28 inches (70 cm)*.

Nezu-Ogon, *32 inches (80 cm)*.

Ginbo (Ghost Koi), *30 inches (75 cm)*.

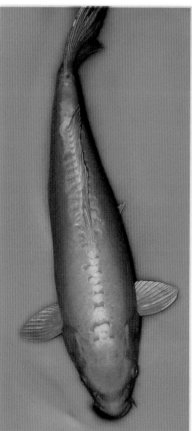

Doitsu Orenji-Ogon, *22 inches (55 cm)*.

Hikari-Moyomono

Moyo is the Japanese word for pattern. This group accommodates all koi with two or more metallic colors. Within *Hikari-Moyomono* we distinguish between *Hariwake*, which has a patchwork pattern of gold and silver, and those that were crossbred from *Ogon* or other varieties (except *Utsurimono*).

In any of the *Hikari-Moyomono* the pattern must be evenly balanced and eye-catching; if it is too light or insufficient it is not acceptable. A strong metallic silver or golden ground easily dominates additional colors and can overpower a pattern, making it hard for other markings to appear thick and strong.

The scalation must be flawless, especially in the *doitsu* variations. An unblemished bald head, with no indication of black smudging or haziness is sought after. The pectoral fins should have good luster.

Hariwake color and pattern types

Hariwake A gold- or silver-patterned koi. The pattern ought to be bold, clear-cut, and balanced across the body. The more *fukurin* on the scalation, the better the *Hariwake* will display its color and pattern qualities.

Yamabuki-Hariwake Inlays of platinum-colored pattern on a ground that is a lemony shade of gold (*yamabuki*). The *doitsu* version shows off the platinum pattern to better advantage.

Orenji-Hariwake The ground is *orenji* (orange-gold) and the pattern is platinum colored. In its *doitsu* form, the orange-gold appears even brighter.

Kikusui The *doitsu* of the *Yamabuki-Hariwake* and *Orengi-Hariwake*, with a wave pattern of yellow, orange, and red-gold that is symmetrically arranged on the flanks.

Matsuba-Hariwake *Hariwake* with *matsuba* scalation.

Kujaku, *18 inches (45 cm).*

Hariwake, *22 inches (55 cm).*

Yamatonishiki, *24 inches (60 cm).*

Specimens with exceptional *fukurin* on the scales of the back are named *Hyakunen-Zamkura*. This version is also bred from *doitsu* Platinum-*Ogon* and *doitsu Kohaku* to produce a better effect and *hi* pattern.

Other color and pattern types

Platinum-*Kohaku* (*Kin-Fuji*) Bred from Platinum-*Ogon* and *Kohaku* to produce a metallic *Kohaku*. The ground color is platinum and the pattern overlay is usually a yellowish red. Specimens with bright red *hi* are now seen more often.

Sakura-Ogon A *Kanoko-Kohaku* (a dappled *hi* pattern) with an overlay of *hikari* luster.

Yamatonishiki The metallic version of *Sanke*. This commonly features a deep hue of *hi* and small, clearly defined *sumi* on a ground of platinum. To appreciate *Yamatoshiniki*, the desired qualities of both *Hariwake* and *Sanke* must be sought.

Kinsui and *Ginsui*

The *Hikarimono* versions of *Shusui. Kinsui* tend to have more *hi* markings and *Ginsui* fewer. The luster on young fish tends to fade as they grow. In *Kinsui* the luster must extend across the body to show off neatly aligned, dark scales on the dorsal line and waves of *hi* on the abdomen, pectoral fins, and cheeks.

Shochikubai A metallic *Aigoromo*, with great rarity value. It requires a regular indigo pattern with luster that covers the head and body and extends to the tips of the pectoral fins.

Gin-Bekko and **Kin-Bekko** Produced out of *Shiro-Bekko* and Platinum-*Ogon* or *Yamabuki-Ogon* as a by-product of *Yamato-nishiki* breeding. The typical *Shiro-Bekko sumi* pattern must appear elevated on the platinum ground.

Tora-Ogon A *Hariwake* with a *sumi* pattern, bred out of *Gin-Bekko/Orenji-Ogon* or *Yamatonishiki/*Platinum-*Ogon* parents. It is difficult to achieve a balance of *hikari* and *sumi* in this fish.

Kin-Bekko, *22 inches (55 cm)*.

Gin-Bekko, *20 inches (50 cm)*.

Tora-Ogon, *20 inches (50 cm)*.

Kujaku (*Kujaku-Ogon*) One of the most impressive of the *Hikari-Moyomono*, *Kujaku* has been described as having the "unique gorgeousness of *Hikarimono*, the rare appearance of *Kawarimono* and an elegant luster and pattern" that combine to create an air of nobility. *Kujaku* originated from breeding a female *Shusui* to *Matsuba-Ogon* and *Hariwake* males, which produced *wagoi* and *doitsu* offspring that featured *sumi* markings resembling the feathers of a peacock.

The base has *Asagi* patterning with platinum luster and an overlay of *hi* markings. If the *hi* covers all the body, it is known as *Beni-Kujaku*. In *doitsu Kujaku* the *matsuba*-style scales on the back are black and the *hi* markings appear to float on the ground color.

The name *"Heisei Nishiki,"* for the scaleless metallic *Sanke* or *doitsu Yamatonishiki*, has gained popularity lately.

Kikusui, *16 inches (40 cm)*.

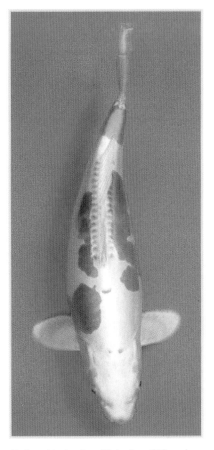
Doitsu Hariwake, *12 inches (30 cm)*.

Kikusui, *20 inches (50 cm)*.

Hikari-Utsurimono

The *Hikari-Utsurimono* results from crossbreeding *Ogon* to *Showa* or *Ogon* to *Utsurimono* to produce *Showa* and *Utsuri* with a metallic sheen. The *Showa* and *Shiro* variations could be either *kin* (golden) or *gin* (silver), but both variations are named *Kin-Showa*.

Breeders have recently improved the strength and quality of the *hi* and *sumi*, which previously appeared as yellow *hi* and blurred, pale *sumi*. An adult *Hikari-Utsurimono* with strong color and pattern is a treasured koi.

This variety has a tendency for *sumi* to fade under stressful situations, such as during transport and handling. At koi shows it is not unusual to see *Hikari-Utsurimono* which were brilliantly colored in their ponds fade to dull gray and insipid gold in response to the stress.

Gold flecking on the *sumi*, shadowy blemishes on the ground color and dull luster rob *Hikari-Utsurimono* of their appeal and value.

Color and pattern types

Kin-Showa A metallic *Showa* with strong golden luster, bred out of *Ogon* and *Showa*.

Gin-Showa A metallic *Showa* with a strong platinum luster.

Gin-Shiro Produced from breeding Platinum-*Ogon* to *Shiro-Utsuri*. The *sumi* pattern on the platinum ground must be bold and solid for maximum effect.

Kin Ki-Utsuri (*Ogon-Utsuri*, *Kin-Shiro*) Produced from introducing *Ogon* to *Ki-Utsuri* or *Hi-Utsuri*.

Gin-Shiro, *14 inches (35 cm).*

Kin-Showa, *16 inches (40 cm).*

Kin Ki-Utsuri, *32 inches (80 cm).*

Tancho

When a round *hi* mark on the head is the only *hi* marking on the body, the koi is grouped under *Tancho*. Traditionally associated with *Kohaku*, *Sanke*, or *Showa*, *tancho* also occurs in the other varieties. A roundish *hi* marking in addition to other *hi* markings is known as *maruten*.

These highly prized koi are named for the Manchurian crane (*Grus japonensis*), a white bird with a red cap. The marking is also reminiscent of the Japanese flag, which shows a red sun (*Hinomaru*) on a white field.

Tancho markings of various shapes (square, diamond, oval, heart, cross, and blossom) are acknowledged but are not as highly prized as the perfect round *hi* marking. The ideal *tancho* mark must be confined to the head and may not touch or extend over the eyes, lips, cheeks, or shoulder. Its position must be in perfect balance to the head and the marking must be thick, even, and bright with sharp *kiwa*. The white ground must be thick, pure, and without any distracting blemishes so that the *tancho* is sharply etched for maximum effect.

Pattern types

Tancho Kohaku A *Kohaku* with the *tancho* as the only *hi* marking. In addition to a perfectly white body, the pectoral fins should be unblemished.

Tancho Sanke A *Sanke* with *tancho* as the only *hi* marking. The *sumi* pattern must be well defined in the desired style for *Shiro-Bekko*. Some *tejima* in the pectoral fins will create balance.

Tancho Showa A *Showa* with *tancho* as the only *hi* marking. A *sumi* head marking must touch or run through the *tancho* without obscuring or spoiling it. The *sumi* pattern must be as for *Showa* or *Shiro-Utsuri*; *motoguro* in the pectoral fins will round off the picture.

Tancho Showa, *10 inches (25 cm).*

Tancho Sanke, *22 inches (55 cm).*

Tancho Kohaku, *23 inches (58 cm).*

Kinginrin

Any type of koi with iridescent scalation along the length of the back, or elsewhere on the body, is classified as *Kinginrin*.

The scale is best described as having a silvery deposit on the surface or edge, but it is actually colorless and transparent with small platelets that reflect light. The scales are arranged in two or more neat rows on both sides of the dorsal line. The silvery type (those on a white ground or on *sumi* markings) is *ginrin* and the golden type (those on *hi*) is *kinrin*.

Many koi have a few shiny scales on their bodies, but to qualify as true *Kinginrin* there must be a minimum of 20 such scales. However, in a good specimen of *Kinginrin* the scalation must be extensive, in perfect alignment and with high sheen and sparkle to each scale.

As such a wide variety of types can exhibit *Kinginrin* characteristics, the basic features of the original type must be present alongside quality *Kinginrin*. The one's strength cannot compensate for the weakness of the other.

For show purposes, *Kinginrin Kohaku*, *Sanke*, *Showa*, and *Utsurimono* are judged separately from the other *Kinginrin* varieties. The former group is known as *Kinginrin* A and the latter as *Kinginrin* B. A distinction is also made between the Niigata and Hiroshima *Kinginrin* scale types.

Though koi are called "living jewels," it is *Kinginrin* that are most worthy of this epithet.

Ginrin Kohaku, *10 inches (25 cm).*

Ginrin Kuro-Goshiki, *22 inches (55 cm).*

Ginrin Tancho Showa, *18 inches (45 cm).*

Niigata *Kinginrin*

Kado-gin, **Sudare-gin**, and **Kasu-gin** Only the posterior edge of the *Kado-gin* scale glitters. In *Sudare-gin* the glitter radiates from the edge to the inner part, and the longer the radiating streaks, the better the quality. The least favored type is *Kasu-gin* (*scum-gin*) which is an irregular arrangement along the edge of the scale.

Tama-gin (Pearl-*Ginrin*, *Tsubo-gin*) The scales have glittering round centers that appear to rise above the surface. This three-dimensional effect creates the impression of strings of pearls. The quality of this *Kinginrin* is lost as the fish grows.

Beta-gin This offers the highest quality of *Kinginrin* because the entire scale is covered in glitter. It commonly occurs scattered over the body, especially along the flanks, and is seldom arranged in rows along the dorsal line.

Hiroshima-*Ginrin*

Hiroshima-*Ginrin*, also known as Hiroshima *Nishiki*, comprises **Dia-gin**, **Chara-gin**, and **Gacha-gin**. In the *Dia-gin* type, each scale looks as if it has diamonds embedded in it. The scales appear in rows along the dorsal line and the reflection can be strong enough to blur the outlines of pattern markings.

If the shine glitters like tinsel or gold leaf it is called *Chara-gin*, and if it appears like cracks, it is referred to as *Gacha-gin*.

Ginrin Kujaku, *14 inches (35 cm)*.

Pearl-Shiromuji, *14 inches (35 cm)*.

Ginrin Showa, *22 inches (55 cm)*.

The water environment

In the wild, carp inhabit natural ponds and lakes, and deep, slow-moving rivers, where they can churn up the bottom soil in search of morsels of food and where the muddy or green water offers them protection from predators.

By contrast, an artificial pond environment, which is home to most koi for the duration of their lives, is usually kept crystal clear so that the fish can be viewed and enjoyed. Therefore, the challenge for koi-keepers is to offer their fish the opportunity to survive and thrive in an artificial pond with its rigid boundaries, limited space, and constantly recirculated water.

Water quality

When we see a pond with crystal-clear water, we perceive the quality of the water as "excellent" whereas if the koi are hidden in a green algal soup, we consider it "poor." However, water quality has to be defined in terms of its intended use. City tap water may be good for drinking but it is completely unsuitable for koi because of its high chlorine content.

Koi are content with mud ponds that are green with algae and alive with microorganisms; they grow and reproduce well here. Although professional koi farmers try to emulate mud dam conditions for optimum reproduction, urban koi-keepers who want to display their collection in its full glory desire water that is crystal clear, free from floating algae and other debris, and has a faint nutty taste and a fresh smell.

For koi-keeping purposes, water quality can be defined as the suitability of the water in any given pond for the rearing and displaying of koi.

In the early days, koi kept in urban ponds often had a very short lifespan. It was only in the mid-1960s that people began to realize that pond water needed to be oxygenated to keep pace with increased koi populations and higher feed rates, that external parasites on the fish had to be controlled, that pond water could be treated to improve its quality, and that adequate water circulation in the replacement of pond-bottom water was important.

Today, with increased knowledge and understanding of water quality parameters, we can create beautiful collections of koi and keep them alive. We understand the consequences for koi if certain minimum water quality conditions are not met, and accept that even minute changes in some water quality parameters will stress the fish, causing a physiological impact that could ultimately result in disease, or even death.

The many properties of water can be broadly divided into three categories, all of which are interdependent:

• Physical—mainly caused by climatic conditions, like temperature, wind, sunlight, altitude, and suspended solids.

• Chemical—these relate to the composition of the water and the minerals that are dissolved in it.

• Biological—these relate to the full spectrum of organic life (derived from animals or plants) in the water.

Whether or not a pond is suitable for koi has more to do with its water quality than any other factor. Given the right water parameters, koi will thrive and grow, but poor water will affect their growth and health in the long run.

When trying to diagnose problematic ponds, there are many variables to take into account. For example, wind can change the turbidity (see page 85), reducing the activity of algae that, in turn, can affect diurnal pH swing (see page 78), and, ultimately, ammonia toxicity (see page 81). Pond owners must be aware of the interdependence of many seemingly unrelated factors, as the ultimate objective is to manage your pond so as to achieve the best result from the blend of chemical, biological, and climatic conditions that is unique to each pond.

For fish, water is the medium in which metabolic and anabolic life-supporting chemical processes take place within the confines of each living cell, between cells and organs within the body, and through the thin gill membranes. The reaction rate of these chemical processes is influenced by physical factors such as temperature or the presence of the right chemical compounds in the right concentrations.

Because of the close relationship between a koi and its watery environment, any change in the physical and chemical makeup of pond water can quickly affect almost any organ in the koi's body.

The rate at which chemicals are dispersed through water is influenced by its natural flow and movement.

Water temperatures

While they prefer stable water, koi are able to tolerate temperatures from freezing to 95°F (35°C), although it is not clear how long they can survive at such extremes. An ideal water temperature range is 68–77°F (20–25°C) in summer for growth, and an extended spell of below 50°F (10°C) in winter to develop body shape. This is based on the seasonal temperature profile of the Niigata Prefecture in Japan, the "home" of koi. However, koi kept in countries with wide-ranging annual temperature fluctuations seem to do fine, as long as local knowledge is applied during the extreme phases of the seasons.

A sudden drop of as little as 4°F (2°C) in water temperature can reduce the koi's ability to fend off parasites that, if untreated, could lead to death. On the other hand, a sharp increase of up to four degrees is usually tolerated okay, although it can trigger parasitic activity.

As water temperature affects both sheen and color, it is particularly relevant when preparing koi for a show. *Hi* and *sumi* improve in depth and intensity and a better finish of the white ground is achieved in water at 50–68°F (10–20°C), while the difference in radiance of hikari koi is remarkable in water of less than 68°F (20°C) when compared with their summer gloss.

Sunlight helps to improve the koi's skin gloss and mucus layer, with the ultraviolet rays stimulating certain sterols in the skin to produce Vitamin D. Too much direct sunlight can do damage, however. Both fading color and the skin disease *hikui* are often blamed on excessive exposure to sunlight, although other factors are probably involved.

Physical factors

Temperature is a major factor in the aquatic environment of the pond. Koi, as well as bacteria, algae, and parasites, are all influenced by the ambient temperature. Like most fish, koi are poikilothermic (cold-blooded) creatures that cannot control their body temperature. Their metabolic rate is entirely dependent on the external water temperature, and, consequently, all their bodily functions—like growth, procreation, aging, and physical activity—are controlled by the external environmental temperature.

Female koi must experience a water temperature of least 62°F (16.8°C) for a sufficient period in order to ovulate and spawn, which is why koi normally breed in spring and early summer, when the water starts to warm up.

A koi's appetite is also affected by water temperature. At 59°F (15°C) it takes one day for food to pass through their gut, while at 52°F (11°C) it takes up to five days. Koi can therefore consume five times more food per day at 59°F than at 52°F, converting it to energy and body mass (i.e. size).

Higher feed intake results in higher oxygen demand, as well as more toxins being excreted into the water. If these conditions are not corrected by the pond filter system, the resulting loss of water quality will suppress the koi's appetite. The solubility of oxygen decreases drastically with increased temperature, while the toxicity of substances like ammonia is increased. An increase in temperature leads to an increase in vigor, activity, feeding, and growth, but can just as easily result in conditions of poor water quality, and suppress the craving for food.

Virtually all the organisms in a pond respond to temperature changes, giving rise to speculation that the different metabolic rates of various organisms is the reason for parasite outbreaks during spring and fall when temperatures tend to fluctuate more than usual.

In the wild, environmental temperatures have an impact on the carp's breeding cycles and development.

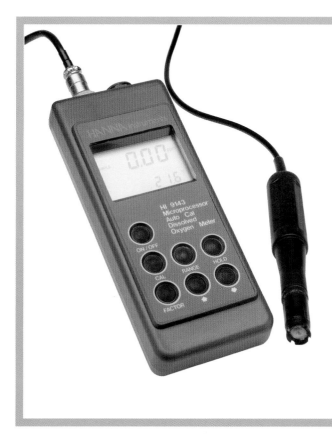

Measuring chemicals in pond water

Electronic meters that measure dissolved oxygen and other chemical components have probes that require proper maintenance and regular calibration. This can be done by means of a simple procedure to ensure meaningful results.

Some of the more expensive meters have additional functions, which differ from manufacturer to manufacturer. Refer to your instruction manual.

Water stratification

Deep ponds without proper water circulation tend to develop horizontal layers of water of equal temperature (thermal stratification). In summer, the bottom water can be cooler than the surface water; while in winter the water at the bottom of the pond may remain warmer if left undisturbed. Koi-keepers in cold regions sometimes use different circulation strategies in winter to blend the warmer bottom water with the colder upper layers.

In addition to thermal stratification, layers of similar chemical makeup and density may also form in undisturbed areas of the pond. Therefore, parts of the pond bottom can become lower in oxygen and may develop anaerobic or anoxic bacterial flora that produce toxic by-products.

To avoid the potentially harmful effects of both thermal and chemical stratification, all pond water should be circulated effectively and bottom drains flushed regularly (see page 93).

Saturation

"Percentage saturation" is the term used to indicate the amount of gas present in water, in terms of the maximum possible concentration of gas at a specific temperature and altitude.

It can be used to give an indicatiwon of how effective the aeration of a pond system should be in order to maintain optimal conditions.

Chemical factors

Water contains many dissolved substances, some of which, like oxygen, dissolve and disperse while maintaining their molecular structure. It is a property of water that many substances important to the processes of life do not only dissolve, but also dissociate into free ions, losing their molecular identity in the process. In this manner, table salt (sodium chloride, NaCl) dissociates into Na+ and Cl– ions, each ion now being able to associate and react with other ions in solution.

Throughout the world, natural waters vary widely, but most contain limited quantities of chemicals, including sodium, calcium, potassium, bicarbonate, and magnesium positive ions in solution, countered by negative ions of chloride, sulfate, carbonate, and nitrate. Small amounts of iron, copper, zinc, and other trace elements may be found in ground water. No matter how small, though, these substances can all influence water quality, with a relatively small shift in some components having a significant effect on overall water quality.

A flowmeter is an effective way of aerating a pond.

The more ions there are present in the water, the higher the conductivity, and the more dissolved solids will be evident when a drop of water evaporates. Water may taste more bitter due to the presence of carbonates, more salty due to chlorides, or become less palatable due to sulfates and nitrates, to a point where it becomes undrinkable.

As long as toxic components are eliminated, koi can do quite well in a wide range of water types, from very soft to mildly salty.

Dissolved oxygen

Koi require oxygen to live. It enables them to convert food, an energy source, into a usable form, which is why oxygen consumption increases dramatically after eating. Oxygen is therefore an important water quality parameter and the main factor limiting aquatic life in a pond. Adequate concentrations of dissolved oxygen (DO) must be maintained in pond water in order to ensure the fish's survival.

Insufficient oxygen has an immediate effect on koi, causing them severe stress. At low, sub-lethal levels of oxygen, the koi will stop eating, become lethargic and soon become infested with parasites. Bacterial infection is likely under these conditions. If oxygen deprivation is severe, the koi will quickly lose consciousness, followed by brain damage and death.

Oxygen dissolves when it comes into contact with the water's surface. It is then dispersed by natural movement or by artificial stirring or pumping. Effective oxygenation can be achieved in ponds by continuously replacing oxygen-saturated surface water with bottom water that is low in oxygen. The solubility of oxygen is influenced by temperature, air pressure, altitude, and salinity. Adequate oxygenation of koi ponds is important at high altitudes and during the summer.

For normal activities, koi require about 880 mg of oxygen per kilogram (2.2 lb) of body mass per hour at 68°F (20°C). Oxygen demand fluctuates during the day, reaching highs after feeding, and dropping when resting. Koi will survive at a dissolved oxygen level of as low as 3 parts per million (ppm), or 3 mg/L, but to ensure growth and a healthy appetite a minimum DO level of 6 ppm (6 mg/L) is required.

Koi-keepers who live in high-temperature and/or high-altitude areas should always consider the combined effects of altitude and temperature on the solubility of oxygen. On a warm day, the aeration strategy must ensure that 100 percent saturation is achieved in order to maintain a comfortable 6 ppm (6 mg/L) DO level.

Aeration methods include waterfalls, air stones driven by air pumps, and flow meters. The latter is an effective way of stirring up the pond water as well as injecting a stream of air into the water. To function properly, flow meters should be installed no deeper than 12 inches (30 cm) under the water.

Oxygen is not only needed by fish, but also by all the biological processes that take place within the pond, including in the filter. If the pond water is aerated by normal means, such as via a waterfall or flowmeter, there can never be too much oxygen and no harm can come to the fish. In fact, an overabundance of oxygen will improve your chance of having a pond with little anaerobic bacterial activity and a reduced risk of disease.

The easiest way to determine the dissolved oxygen content of pond water is to use an electronic meter designed for this purpose (see page 75).

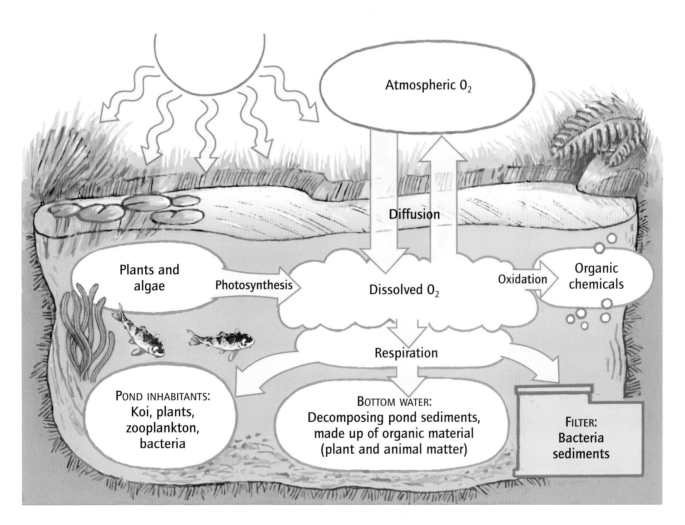

Atmospheric oxygen dissolves readily at the point of contact with water, but then disperses more slowly through the pond. Pumping or stirring the water helps to bring oxygen-depleted bottom water into contact with the oxygen-rich water at the surface.

pH

As a measure of the acidity or alkalinity of water, the pH expresses the concentration of hydrogen ions in a water sample on a logarithmic scale from 0–14 with 7 being the neutral point. Pure water (H_2O) is pH neutral.

As minerals dissolve in water the equilibrium shifts. An increase in the amount of hydrogen ions makes water more acidic, while a decrease makes it more alkaline.

The pH is often misunderstood. A pH of 7.0 may be perfect, according to many, but it may be unsuitable for fish because of, say, the lack of calcium or buffering capacity. pH should be seen in context with all the constituents of a water sample. It is not so much the pH itself that is crucial, but the ionic content giving rise to the pH. It is only at the extremes that pH is a true indicator of real trouble.

Like many other fish, koi have a remarkable tolerance for pH extremes and can even acclimatize to acidic water with pH as low as 4.5. In mud ponds, koi can withstand a diurnal (daily) pH swing, due to photosynthesis, that may range over three

Dip a test strip into the pond water to check the pH level.

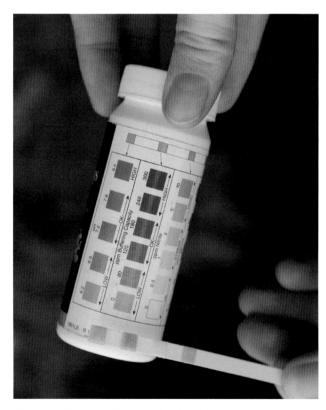

Compare the specially treated strip with the color charts.

pH units and may reach levels as high as 10.0. At the extremes of pH, the presence of other chemical constituents in the water become more critical for survival. The toxicity of ammonia, copper, and iron are all affected by pH. A pH of 7.5 to 8.3 represents water that is well-buffered and less likely to have toxic effects from heavy metals (but not from ammonia).

Koi are probably not very sensitive to pH swing, and can handle a range of pH 5.0-9.0 with ease, but they do react to the chemical interactions that cause changes in pH levels. A low pH tends to favor *sumi* development, while a higher pH is better for the *hi* and for skin tone.

There are times when the pH of pond water may need to be adjusted. Before doing so, koi-keepers should know the cause of the imbalance. Recently built concrete and mortar ponds may be too alkaline due to the leaching of cement, while ponds made from synthetic resins may be too acidic. If the pH is wrong, newly introduced fish will most likely die.

If flushing and refilling the pond is not an option, the pH can be adjusted artificially, using one of the many proprietary treatments available. It is advisable not to use any containing phosphates or nitrates, as they can provide fertilizer for algae. If the pH measures 7.5-8.3, it is preferable to leave the water alone. Adding chemicals to a pond is always potentially hazardous and should be avoided whenever possible.

In mature ponds, the pH tends to drift downward due to the activity of nitrifying bacteria. This "acid creep" must be treated on an ongoing basis with a good carbonate source, such as scallop or oyster shells, coral rock (aragonite), or regular water changes (up to 10 percent) with municipal tap water.

Alternatively, sodium bicarbonate (baking soda, $NaHCO_3$) can be used at a ratio of a flat to heaped teaspoon (5-10 g) per 264 gallons (1,000 L) pond water per day until the desired pH is reached. However, this treatment only replenishes lost alkalinity, not any calcium (hardness) flushed out as the remains of dead bacteria.

Oyster shells are a natural source of calcium and can be used to rectify water imbalances.

The addition of coral rock/aragonite (top) or dolomite (above) helps to buffer pond water against pH extremes.

Carbon dioxide, alkalinity, and hardness

The relationship between carbon dioxide, carbonate, and calcium/magnesium in the pH buffering system helps to maintain (i.e., minimize) the steady, diurnal (daily) pH fluctuation. In recirculating pond systems, measures must be taken to replenish both calcium and carbonate ions. Alkalinity (carbonate) helps to protect the water from fast and sudden pH drops, while hardness (calcium) helps to protect it from fast and sudden pH increases.

Carbon dioxide Dissolved in water, carbon dioxide (CO_2) forms part of a natural buffer system that keeps a pond's pH relatively stable. It is also important for photosynthesis and respiration, and is the source of carbon, the element at the base of all organic life processes. Most pond water has a limited supply of carbonates which, in turn, are influenced by bacteria and algae that consume carbon by actively removing carbonates from the water during nitrification (see page 82), resulting in a loss of its buffering capacity. To counter this, carbonate sources, such as oyster shells or limestone chips, can be added to the pond.

Alkalinity Bicarbonate, carbonate, hydroxide, ammonia, phosphate, and silicate ions contribute alkalinity to water. Total alkalinity, the concentration of all these ions in solution, is a measure of the degree to which pond water is buffered against pH changes. Between pH 5.4 and 8.3 alkalinity is primarily in the form of bicarbonates. Above pH 8.3, carbonate and bicarbonate ions are both present, while below pH 5.4, water has no alkalinity.

The alkalinity of natural water (rain, river, or spring water) varies depending on the rainfall received, with temperate areas having lower values than arid areas. Water with a total alkalinity between 20 and 120 parts per million (20 and 120mg/L) is best for fish; with the recommended alkalinity for koi ponds being not less than 20 ppm (20mg/L) of equivalent calcium carbonate ($CaCO_3$).

The easiest way to raise alkalinity quickly is to add sodium bicarbonate (¾ oz per 264 gallons) to achieve an increase of about 10 ppm (10mg/L) in alkalinity. In the absence of natural carbonates, like oyster shells, test regularly for alkalinity and remedy accordingly. Avoid quick, large changes and monitor the effect of the treatment after a few hours.

Hardness The presence of limestone and dolomite adds to the pH stability of natural waters. Carbonic acid is a weak acid that readily reacts with insoluble carbonate-containing rock, putting both calcium and bicarbonate ions in solution and thereby helping to buffer the water against high pH extremes. Total hardness is the concentration of calcium and magnesium ions in the water expressed in parts per million (ppm) or milligrams per liter (mg/L) of equivalent calcium carbonate. Hardness is thus a measure of the ability of the water to withstand pH increases.

Ammonia

Fish continuously flush ammonia from their blood via the gills. Ammonia is a waste product of their diet, but it is toxic, and an increase in the concentration of ammonia in the water will impede the process of ammonia removal and increase the level of ammonia in the blood and tissues.

The amount of ammonia produced is proportional to the amount of protein a koi consumes. Food with a 35 percent protein content produces about 12.7 gram of ammonia for every pound of food digested (see table below).

AMMONIA LOADING AS A RESULT OF FEEDING QUALITY FOODS WITH VARIOUS PROTEIN CONTENT	
PROTEIN CONTENT OF FEED (%)	APPROX. AMMONIA PRODUCED (GRAM NH_3 PER POUND FOOD)
25	9.1
30	10.9
35	12.7
40	14.5
45	16.3
50	18.2

Ammonia is a gas that readily dissolves in water, where it is partly ionized to form ammonium ions. The relative abundance of toxic unionized ammonia ions is determined by the pH and temperature of the pond water. As test kits cannot distinguish between ionized and unionized ammonia, they give the total ammonia, which is the sum of the unionized (NH_3) and ionized (NH_4^+) ions in solution. Knowing the pH and water temperature helps determine the ammonia toxicity of pond water (see table below).

Exposure to ammonia levels as low as 0.5ppm (0.5mg/L) results in discomfort for fish. They become stressed, their gill filaments swell and they become an easy target for bacterial infection. Long-term exposure to levels of unionized ammonia exceeding 0.02ppm (0.02mg/L) is detrimental to koi, retarding their growth and increasing their susceptibility to disease. Every effort should be made to maintain a total ammonia level as close to zero as possible, because even ionized ammonia can have a negative long-term effect on fish health.

Any sign of ammonia in a pond should be investigated. High pH levels call for immediate action. If the pH is 7.0 or less, there is no need to panic, but the problem should be rectified as soon as possible.

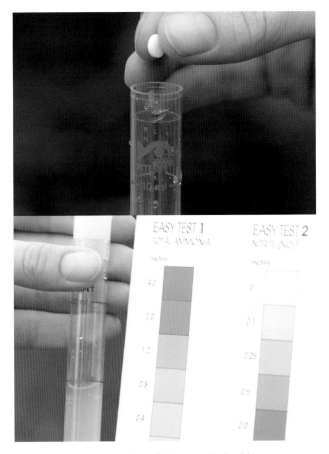

To test for total ammonia, add the required tablets to a water sample, allow them to dissolve, and compare the resulting color with the indicator chart.

PERCENTAGE OF UNIONIZED AMMONIA IN WATER AT DIFFERENT TEMPERATURES AND PH VALUES							
pH	46°F (8°C)	54°F (12°C)	61°F (16°C)	68°F (20°C)	75°F (24°C)	82°F (28°C)	90°F (32°C)
7.0	0.2	0.2	0.3	0.4	0.5	0.7	1.0
8.0	1.6	2.1	2.9	3.8	5.0	6.6	8.8
8.2	2.5	3.3	4.5	5.9	7.7	10.0	13.2
8.4	3.9	5.2	6.9	9.1	11.6	15.0	19.
8.6	6.0	7.9	10.6	13.7	17.3	21.8	27.7
8.8	9.2	12.0	15.8	20.1	24.9	30.7	37.8
9.0	13.8	17.8	22.9	28.5	34.4	41.2	49.0
9.2	20.4	25.8	32.0	38.7	45.4	52.6	60.4
9.4	30.0	35.5	42.7	50.0	56.9	63.8	70.7
9.6	39.2	46.5	54.1	61.3	67.6	73.6	79.3
10.0	61.7	68.5	74.8	79.9	84.0	87.5	90.6
10.2	71.9	77.5	82.4	86.3	98.3	91.8	93.8

Treating ammonia

Ammonia concentration can be determined with colorimetric test kits which compare a color reaction with a paper chart to get an ammonia reading. These kits are cheap, and no koi-keeper should be without one. More accurate results can be obtained from electronic colorimeters that are standardized for ammonia measurements.

When toxic levels of ammonia are found, immediate action is needed. Stop feeding the fish and do an initial 50 percent water change. Do a follow-up measurement and change more water if this is needed. Keep some zeolite handy for an emergency, as it quickly and effectively removes ammonia by the process of ion exchange. Zeolite can be reactivated for future use by treating it with concentrated salt solution that will dispel the ammonia.

Sulfonate products, which neutralize ammonia instantly by forming the stable substance aminomethanesulfonate, are also useful in an emergency, as well as at koi shows or when starting up a new pond. (Using sulfonate products will make ammonia tests inaccurate for a time.)

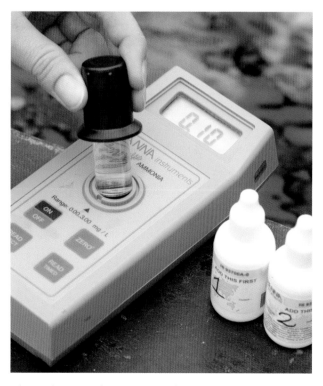

Electronic ammonia test meters give accurate results.

In order to treat a pond successfully, the reason for the increased ammonia must be established and the problem rectified, as chemical treatments are expensive to maintain over any length of time.

Ammonia-related problems are most likely to be caused by overstocking, or by a dramatic increase in the koi population, coupled with ineffective filtration, too low water turnover rate (see page 96), overfeeding, seasonal temperature changes, or simply unhygienic pond conditions.

The nitrogen cycle

This is a series of natural processes to preserve and recycle nitrogen, a basic nutrient utilized by all living organisms. Earth's atmosphere is a vast source of nitrogen, but plant and animal life also have a huge store of it embedded in their structure in a complex organic form. The nitrogen cycle ensures that nitrogen is not permanently lost for organic life.

There are many different processes driving the cycle. From a koi-keeper's perspective, the most important are ammonification, mineralization, nitrification, and denitrification.

Proteins are an essential part of koi food. They are complex organic molecules that, when digested, are reduced to simple amino acids that are used as building blocks to grow new tissue, as well as "fuel" to provide energy for cellular processes.

In the process of ammonification, fish use oxygen to oxidize amino acids to meet their growth requirements. Ammonia and carbon dioxide are produced as waste products and excreted via the gills. An uncontrolled increase in natural ammonia is dangerous for fish but, during the process of nitrification, microbial organisms obtain nutrition by oxidizing ammonia and turning it to nitrate in a two-step process.

Nitrification converts toxic ammonia to relatively nontoxic nitrate. The process consumes alkaline elements, decreases pH, and produces carbon dioxide. Ammonia is first oxidized to nitrite which, in turn, is oxidized to nitrates.

For this to occur, oxygen is required and the concentration of hydrogen ions increases. *Nitrosomonas* bacteria are most commonly associated with the first stage of nitrification and

Nitrobacter with the second. By oxidizing ammonia and consuming carbon, a microbial biomass is grown.

Oxygen is required at a rate of 3.5 mg and bicarbonate at 8.7 mg for every milligram of ammonia that is converted to nitrate. The process is sensitive to both temperature and pH changes. Higher pH levels increase the rate at which ammonia is converted to nitrite, but decrease the oxidizing rate at which nitrite is converted to nitrate. If the water temperature is high, the entire process is speeded up.

Nitrifying bacteria produce 170 mg of cell mass for each gram of ammonium-nitrogen oxidized. Fortunately, this is a relatively small amount when compared with that produced by heterotrophic bacteria, resulting in less mass to clog biological filters. *Nitrosomonas* and *Nitrobacter* are among the most prevalent species of nitrobacteria in pond systems, but other species, even some fungi, have been found to be nitrifiers.

Under anaerobic (nonoxygen-dependent) conditions the process is reversed; bacteria in need of oxygen reduce nitrates to nitrites and ultimately to ammonia or nitrogen gas. Denitrification is an important link in the nitrogen cycle in nature, but it can have a negative, and potentially lethal, effect on the water quality if it occurs in the confines of a home pond.

Although nitrification is employed with great effect in biological filters (see page 99), it creates two problems in pond management. When a new pond is populated, microbial flora do not always react fast enough to the increased ammonia build-up, leaving the fish exposed to higher ammonia levels than they can withstand, while the high demand for oxygen during this process can cause anoxic conditions (lacking in oxygen), preventing further stages in nitrification.

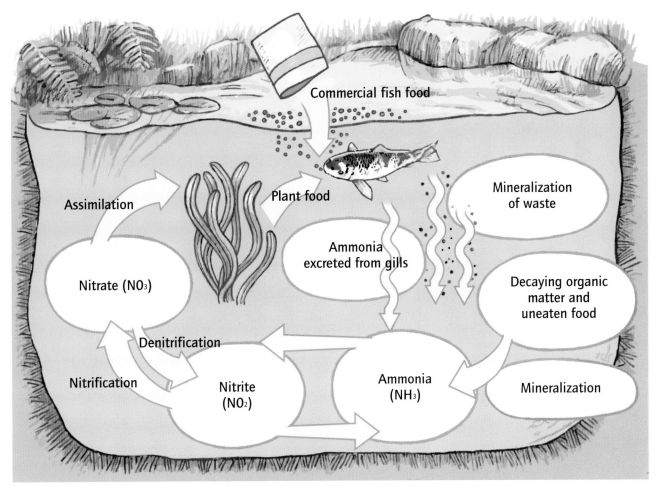

The nitrogen cycle is nature's way of recycling nitrogen, a basic nutrient of living organisms, so that it can be reused.

Nitrate build-up can be reduced by introducing plants, such as water iris, with a good root system that can act as a biological filter, helping to clean water of impurities (take care that koi don't eat the roots!)

Nitrite

Nitrite is a product of the oxidation of ammonia during the nitrification process. In anaerobic conditions nitrites can also be formed by the reduction of nitrates by certain bacteria. Nitrites can cause trouble in newly established ponds and in poorly designed filter systems.

Nitrites are toxic because when they are absorbed into fish blood they oxidize hemoglobin to methemoglobin, reducing the blood's oxygen-carrying capacity. When this happens, the gills typically turn brown, giving rise to the term "brown blood disease" for nitrite poisoning. Continous exposure to sub-lethal levels of nitrite stresses fish and eventually makes them susceptible to bacterial and fungal gill diseases.

Due to the interaction of various ions in the uptake process of nitrites by the gills, safe levels of nitrites can vary from 0.1ppm (0.1mg/L) in soft water to a maximum of 0.2ppm (0.2mg/L) in hard water.

Testing for nitrites is easy and inexpensive. When you install a new filter system, make sure you have a nitrite test kit handy.

As the filters mature, the onset of a nitrite peak can be very sharp and sudden. A rapid increase in nitrites can be dealt with by partial water changes and adding either salt (NaCl) or calcium chloride ($CaCl_2$) to counter the toxic effect of nitrite.

A surface water change helps to diffuse nutrients.

Nitrate

Nitrate is the product of the nitrification process and continues to increase in concentration over time. Water quality deteriorates as the ion content increases, although the water may not be toxic to fish. At first, the effect will be much like adding salt and reducing osmotic stress for the fish, but at elevated levels of nitrate the water will become "rough," "hard," and bitter. Ideally, nitrate should not exceed 200 ppm (200mg/L).

Although fish may not be harmed, high nitrate levels may have other serious consequences. Nitrate is ideal fertilizer for algae, and an algal bloom turning the pond into "pea soup" overnight can create conditions for an algal die-off when the nutrient source is depleted. The result can be an oxygen-starved pond system, with immediate and dire consequences for the fish population and the filter function.

When anaerobic conditions are created in poorly designed pond systems, nitrates can be reduced to toxic nitrites, resulting in a nitrite "background" that seems difficult to eradicate.

Other than regular water changes, a good solution is to add a "vegetable filter" to the pond. Growing plants like water iris, which have a good root system, somewhere in the water flow where the koi will not be able to chew on them, is an effective and eco-friendly way of dealing with nitrate build-up.

Hydrogen sulfide

Sulfides are produced by certain bacteria under anaerobic conditions. Areas where organic waste settles, like the pond floor or drains, are susceptible because there is usually little water movement, allowing anoxic conditions to prevail.

Sulfides come in different ionic forms depending on the pH of the water. At lower pH levels they are mostly present in the form of hydrogen sulfide, which is lethal to adult fish at levels as low as 0.04ppm (0.04mg/L); interfering with their respiration at cellular level, causing symptoms of hypoxia (oxygen deficiency), an increased ventilation (breathing) rate, and, initially, increased activity as they seek to escape from the toxic environment.

All areas of undisturbed organic waste have the potential to create anaerobic conditions as a microcosm of anaerobic organisms goes about its business of waste disposal. Small quantities of sulfurous and nitrogenous by-products continuously ooze from these areas, but any disturbance can cause significant quantities, even bubbles, of rotten-egg-smelling hydrogen sulfide (H_2S) to escape.

Sensible pond hygiene, regular flushing of bottom drains, and removing sludge are important in order to limit the potential for hydrogen sulfide poisoning. Filter beds that have been disturbed, or sand filters that are backwashed, should be rinsed properly to remove waste.

Although not often found, under-gravel biological filters are particularly susceptible to disturbance. Mass die-offs have been known to occur as a result of someone walking over the gravel bed to maintain the pump.

Turbidity and suspended solids

Turbidity is the decreased ability of water to transmit light due to suspended particles. It is normally indicative of poor circulation, or bad pond or filter design. The "murky water" effect is caused by microscopic organic particles originating from uneaten food, fecal matter, and other organic sources, including algae, that stay suspended in the water.

Other than pond water losing clarity, turbidity has some serious implications for water quality. Suspended debris and dead algae add to the biological oxygen demand, increasing the burden on the oxygen supply and raising the count of heterotrophic bacteria which could lead to infections. Microscopic parasites like *Trichodina* (see page 130), which thrive in murky conditions, can be controlled by reducing turbidity.

There are natural clays and synthetic polymer products on the market that flocculate the suspended particles, enabling them to be removed by mechanical means or via the flushing underground drains. The treatment will be short term, however, unless the source of the turbidity is removed.

There are no guidelines regarding acceptable levels of turbidity for koi ponds. Turbidity that harbors bacteria is obviously unacceptable, but suspended minerals and microscopic algae should not have a negative impact on koi health.

Although heavy metals are not normally a problem in ponds, you should still monitor the water occasionally.

Heavy metals

This term generally refers to elements like aluminum, iron, copper, manganese, mercury, and so on, that are found in free or ionic form in surface or ground water. Although pollution is frequently the cause, they also dissolve in natural water when it permeates through mineral-rich soil.

Most heavy metals are not a major problem in pond aquaculture. Even iron, a common constituent of ground water, is less toxic than was traditionally believed; concentrations of up to 1ppm (mg/L) have no ill effect on fish in well-oxygenated water. (River water is sometimes brown due to a high concentration of nontoxic organic iron complexes, found in the soil.)

Copper, however, is highly toxic to fish because it binds to their gills, disrupting their normal ion-regulatory functions. The toxicity of copper is very sensitive to alkalinity, pH, hardness, and the presence of organic compounds in the water.

Heavy metals can be found in well water, so conduct tests before using these types of water in koi ponds. It is possible to construct filters to reduce iron, manganese, and aluminum and it is always a good practice to aerate ground water vigorously before use.

TOXICITY OF VARIOUS HEAVY METALS TO AQUATIC LIFE	
METAL	**SAFE LIMIT (MG/L, PPM)**
Aluminum	0.1mg/L (0.1ppm)
Cadmium	0.01 (0.01)
Chromium	0.1 (0.1)
Copper	0.025 (0.025)
Iron	0.5 (0.5)
Lead	0.1 (0.1)
Mercury	0.0001 (0.0001)
Manganese	0.1 (0.1)
Nickel	0.1 (0.1)
Zinc	0.1 (0.1)

Chlorine and chloramine

Chlorine is an effective, widely used disinfectant. Municipal authorities commonly use chlorine gas to disinfect household water and ensure it is bacteria-free. Tap water typically has a chlorine content of between 0.3 and 0.8ppm (0.3 and 0.8mg/L). Because chlorine dissipates quickly, it is often combined with ammonia to form chloramine, which is more stable and effective in lower concentrations. As chloramine slowly dissociates, both free chlorine and ammonia are released. Therefore, koi-keepers who use tap water to top up their ponds run the danger of adding ammonia to their pond water as well as prolonging the toxic effect of the chlorine.

Chlorine has a rapid, destructive effect on the gill filaments at levels as low as 0.3ppm (0.3mg/L), causing fish to gasp for air at the surface and ultimately die. Even prolonged exposure to chlorine levels as low as 0.003ppm (0.003mg/L) will inflame gill tissue, making the fish susceptible to bacterial infection of the gills.

Chlorine is a major cause of mortalities in urban koi ponds because its toxicity is ignored or overlooked when the pond is filled with municipal tap water. This can be avoided by dosing with any of the proprietary products available from koi outlets to neutralize chlorine in pond water. Some of the more sophisticated water-conditioning products also remove chloramines and heavy metals at the same time.

Chlorine can be removed with the aid of crystalline sodium thiosulfate (3.8 g per 100 gallons/10 g per 1,000 L of pond water), or by replacing some of the pond water (never more than 50 percent of the total) during cleaning, or when backwashing the filters. At this rate, the organic load in the pond will assist in quickly neutralizing the chlorine.

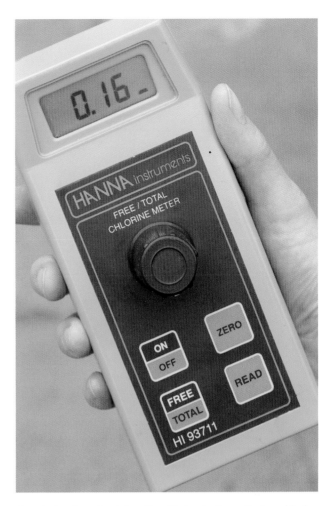

An electronic meter takes the effort out of monitoring chlorine levels in pond water.

To neutralize chlorine

If you do not have a water purifier connected to your water supply then, using a bucket, dissolve the equivalent of about $1/2$ teaspoon (3.8 g) of crystalline sodium thiosulfate per 100 gallon (380 L) of pond water. Pour the solution into the pond. Then dilute about $1/2$ teaspoon (3.5 ml) of 35 percent formalin per 100 gallon (380 L) and add this to the pond to detoxify the chloramines.

Biological factors

The biological factor with the most profound impact on a pond's water quality is the koi collection itself. The only water quality parameter that is defined according to man's needs, and with which koi do not agree, is clarity. Koi thrive in muddy water and they don't mind water rich in algal growth.

Algae

As one of the most fundamental life forms on earth, algae were probably responsible for the creation of our oxygen-rich atmosphere. Algae come in a variety of forms and sustain many organisms at the bottom of the food chain.

Algae are chlorophyll-containing plants that synthesize carbohydrates from basic inorganic nutrients in the presence of sunlight. Some cells in clustered algae may be specialized to fix nitrogen directly from the atmosphere, while others are specialized to reproduce by means of spore formation.

Algae can cause havoc in koi ponds due to the nutrient-rich water. Both single, free-floating cells and multicellular clusters of cells give water a "pea soup" appearance. Large filamentous growths can form long strands that clog pumps and ensnare small fish. Floating wads of blanket weed are unsightly and never enhance a pond.

Some algae smell peculiar (the microscopic algae *Anabaena* emits an odor similar to that of organophosphates) while others, such as spirulina, can be a valuable food source. But algae have one aspect in their favor. Their growth is limited by the least available nutrient, so competition for nutrients can cause some algae to outcompete others. Algal problems can thus be reduced by growing together those algae and plants that are beneficial. A carpet of filamentous algae on the sides of the pond will help remove surplus nutrients from the water, limiting opportunities for micro-algae to become established as "green soup." If the feeding rate is kept low, the koi will continuously harvest the carpet growth, improving the overall balance in the pond.

Algal growth in ponds can supply a rich source of nutrients, but must be kept in balance to ensure the health of your koi.

Minimum Water Quality Conditions

PARAMETER	MINIMUM	MAXIMUM	UNIT
Alkalinity (total alkalinity, as $CaCO_3$)	20	150	ppm
Ammonia (unionized)		0.02	ppm
Carbon dioxide (free total CO_2)		3	ppm
Chlorine (total)		0.003	ppm
Hardness (total hardness as $CaCO_3$)	80	300	ppm
Hydrogen sulfide		0.001	ppm
Nitrite (soft water)		0.1	ppm
Nitrite (hard water)		0.2	ppm
Nitrate		200	ppm
Oxygen (dissolved oxygen)	6% sat.	300% sat.	ppm
pH range (preferred)	7.5	8.3	
pH range (extreme)	6.0	9.0	
Sodium chloride		22.8	g/gallon
Temperature (preferred)	74 (23)	77 (25)	°F (°C)
Temperature (extremes)	32 (0)	95 (35)	°F (°C)

The koi pond

A koi pond is a permanent feature of a garden. Where it is situated and how it blends in will depend on the available space and your own sense of esthetics. Some koi-keepers construct elaborate garden features to show off their collection, but it is possible to rear show-winning koi in a limited pond environment.

Once you have decided to build a proper koi pond, take time to evaluate your property, your lifestyle, and what you want from your koi collection. Making the wrong decision could be costly, so seek advice from fellow koi enthusiasts, garden design specialists, and professional koi dealers before taking the plunge.

Your pond will be around for a considerable time, so make it something you are proud of, and which will add value to your property.

Potential koi owners dream of fish lazily swimming in crystal-clear water when not seeking shade under a canopy of water lily leaves, or a waterfall that scatters sunlight and soothes the soul with its soft gurgle. Too often, they have a rude awakening when the pond water turns into "pea soup," choked by wads of floating blanketweed or string algae, with the fish huddling on the bottom, their misery obvious.

The typical garden pond is quite small and shallow. A DIYer can construct it from bricks, stone, cement, or fiberglass, or by simply lining a hole in the ground with waterproof PVC plastic or butyl rubber. The edges may be formed with stone slabs, rocks, or wooden poles to blend in with the rest of the garden. Those opting for a quick solution can visit a nursery to choose a prefabricated pond in almost any shape and size. Once installed, just fill it with water, add a potted water lily, an ornamental fountain squirting water, a few koi from the local pet store, and you have a pond. Or do you?

Garden ponds may be a source of happy childhood memories, but if you intend to invest in a koi collection, you need to understand their rather exacting requirements so that you can create a perfect environment.

A tranquil pond is the goal of most koi-keepers; regular monitoring and maintenance are the keys to accomplishing this.

Principles of koi pond design

When it comes to koi ponds, size does count. Along with water quality, size—more specifically, depth—is the key to creating the perfect pond. Soil composition, weather conditions, and water properties vary throughout the world, as do construction materials and methods but, wherever you live, the basic requirements for building a good koi pond remain the same.

Site

If you can, position the pond so it does not receive too much sun during the summer months, but gets much-needed sunlight in the winter. Elevated temperatures can make life uncomfortable for your koi, while too little sun in winter will cause the water temperature to drop below what they can comfortably tolerate (see page 73).

Sunlight can have a positive effect on the koi's health. A good guideline is that three to four hours of direct sunlight in the morning will bring out their best, but too much sun, according to some experts, appears to harm skin quality and color, especially the *hi*.

Avoid trees that drop leaves, flowers, fruit, or seeds. Not only will cleaning up become a source of endless frustration, but some plant material is toxic to fish.

Take into consideration the lie of the land and any slope. Think about what will happen if it rains hard or when the snow thaws. If you live in an area where acid rain occurs, or use an irrigation system to deliver plant fertilizers and pesticides to your garden, then chemical pollution is a real risk and preventative measures must be taken.

Whether you dig the pond by hand or use excavating equipment, you will have a mountain of soil that must be removed or relocated. A 30-ton pond will leave you with over 1,000 cubic feet of soil and stone to dispose of.

Drainage

All ponds need to be flushed from time to time, so make provision for removing the waste water. If possible, drain the water downhill or use it to irrigate your garden. In some urban areas, flushing waste water onto the road or into stormwater drains is prohibited and you might have to include a connection to the sewer system.

Utilities

Consider the availability of and access to utilities, including water. Electricity is required to run the pumps and other equipment. In winter, you may need oil or gas to heat the pond. Water, electricity, and natural gas connections must be properly installed without skimping on safety, and should be easily accessible for maintenance and repair. Hire approved contractors to install all the required utilities to the applicable standards for your area.

Avoid trees that drop leaves unless you want to spend hours netting them, as decaying matter will affect water quality.

Design style

There is no prescribed style for a koi pond. A formal pond with straight lines, square angles, and tiled edges is a good option as an extension to a house or when the available space is limited. An informal pond with a freeform design is normally part of the garden and is edged with rocks and plants.

Although a pond can be an expression of your own creativity, whatever its shape, it should not be too narrow relative to the size of the fish you intend to keep.

Surface area

When it comes to size, the availability of garden space and the restrictions on your budget will be limiting factors. A pond with a surface area of 160–320 square feet (15–30 m²) is sufficient for most hobbyists.

The larger the surface area, the larger the air–water interface, which allows more oxygen to be dissolved and more unwanted gases to be released into the atmosphere. Large surface areas also promote significant temperature fluctuation. More heat is absorbed from the sun during the day, but more

Calculating pond capacity

The capacity, or volume, of your pond is the total amount of water it can hold (in gallons or liters). You'll frequently use this figure when making water changes, or calculating the amount of chemicals or treatment products to add, so ensure you are familiar with it from the start.

Pond capacity can be calculated by multiplying surface area (length x width) with the average depth, to get the volume in cubic feet or meters.

For example, a pond with a capacity of 530 cubic feet (15 m³) has a capacity of 3,960 gallons (15,000 L), while a 1,412 cubic feet (40 m³) pond has a capacity of 10,560 gallons (40,000 L).

heat is lost during cold nights. This potentially stressful condition for fish can be minimized by increasing the pond depth and, consequently, the volume of water.

Large koi ponds should be deep enough to minimize the natural daily temperature fluctuations of the pond water.

Pond depth

A depth of at least 5 feet (1.5 m) is recommended for large koi. Avoid ponds less than 4 feet (1.2 m) deep because of the potentially severe fluctuations in water temperature. Koi swim both vertically and horizontally, so depth gives them space to exercise, freedom of movement, and the opportunity to live a more comfortable and stress-free life.

How many fish?

The number and size of fish in your collection is an important factor when planning a pond. There is no simple calculation for this because of the variable relationship between koi body mass (weight), water temperature, water flow rate, filter effectiveness, oxygen availability, and the amount of food the koi consume. A general guideline is to stock the pond with no more than 6.5 pounds (3 kg) of fish body mass per 35 cubic feet (1 m^3) of water.

Koi grow quite fast, and are able to quickly grow to about 22 inches (55 cm) in length. Over time, you will want to add new fish, so bear in mind that a full-grown koi weighs, on average, 7.7 pounds (3.5 kg), and stock the pond accordingly.

The number of fish a pond can cope with is related to its size and depth; overstocking results in poor pond conditions.

Don't forget that, apart from the cost of building, bigger ponds have higher maintainance and running costs. More fish also mean spending more money on food and health care.

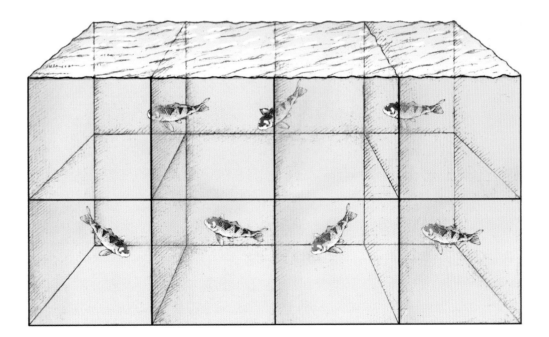

The number of koi a pond can hold is determined by the amount of space each fish requires, according to its size.

Water parameters

Although water quality is discussed more fully in Chapter 4, there are some water parameters that are integral to the creation of a new koi pond.

Turnover rate

While digesting the nutrients in their food, koi consume oxygen and excrete ammonia, feces, and carbon dioxide into the water. For every pound (0.45 kg) of dry food consumed, a koi can excrete 5 pounds (2.3 kg) of solid wet waste, along with nitrogenous waste in the form of ammonia and phosphorus.

An added burden is the oxygen demand placed on the pond's ecosystem. A continuous supply of "fresh" water is required to dilute the polluted water, remove solid waste, and bring oxygen to the pond. Therefore, no matter how small, a pond needs a pump to circulate and aerate the water, which would otherwise become stale and collect an unsightly layer of dust on the surface.

The health of your koi collection is largely determined by the relationship between the rate at which the pond water is diluted by fresh water (the water flow rate) and the residual ammonia load (the amount of ammonia dissolved in the water). This is called the turnover rate. The faster the water is refreshed, the lower the concentration of residual ammonia. If the turnover rate is too slow, the ammonia levels will rise—with dire consequences for the fish. The ideal flow rate results in an effective pond turnover of once every hour, but never slower than once every three hours.

An indoor pond in a stylish setting; no matter where your pond is situated, it is important for your koi's health to maintain a turnover of clean water through the filter.

Bacteria

Millions of bacteria colonies populate the inner surfaces of the pond. Different types of bacteria thrive on various sources of energy, such as fish excrement or decaying plant matter, making them essential for the well-being of any pond.

Heterotrophic bacteria seek out organic compounds to digest for their energy requirements. Nitrifying bacteria thrive on nitrogen-based compounds like ammonia, the removal of which is crucial to the koi's health.

A scrubbed inner surface of a pond is like freshly plowed farmland, on which the first thing to appear is an overabundance of fast-growing weeds. Over time, different plants find a niche by competing for their share of the available nutrient resources. The same applies to bacteria in a pond. Fast-growing heterotrophic bacteria will immediately thrive, but the much-needed, slow-growing nitrifying bacteria will eventually outgrow them and establish a rich diversity of bacterial life.

One of the biggest challenges of the artificial environment we create when we build a pond is to maintain a beneficial diversity of bacterial life. Proper water turnover and flow has a profound effect on bacteria, which are harmed by regular cleaning and disinfecting. The importance of a healthy crop of bacteria for the well-being of a pond cannot be overestimated. Bacteria need both oxygen and a food source to thrive. This is achieved via a collection of fish in a pond with moving, oxygen-rich water, but it cannot be created instantaneously. A koi pond needs to see the cycle of all four seasons before it can be considered mature.

Drains, pumps, and filters

No matter what the design or size of your koi pond, there are a few essential items it should never be without.

Bottom drain Water is removed for recycling via one or more drains in the bottom of the pond. Solids settle where there is the least water movement, so this is where the suction must take place. The drains should be positioned so that all debris and solid fish waste is efficiently removed.

Debris can also be removed by vacuuming the pond bottom, but this is a time-consuming exercise..

Pumps A water pump is the heart of a koi pond. It circulates the water for destratification, oxygenation, and filtration. The pump draws water through the filter and returns it to the pond, ensuring continuous mixing. Some form of aeration (such as a waterfall or flow meter) must be used simultaneously to reoxygenate the water. A well-directed jet of water can be most effective in creating a current and can even be used to move solid wastes towards the drain.

A gravity-fed pond design, where the pump is positioned after the filtration unit, is ideal and can boost final water quality. This set up ensures that fecal matter and food waste are not churned by the pump into microscopic particles that are impossible to settle out by gravitation.

Only pumps rated for continuous operation should be used for koi ponds. The pump must be strong enough to deliver the flow rate your pond requires, turning over all the water every one to two hours. The delivery capacity of a pump is closely related to its power consumption. During the conversion of electrical energy to kinetic energy by the pump motor, energy is always lost due to heat and friction.

Waterfalls reoxygenate and aerate the water, but they may not be sufficient for large fish populations.

Sophisticated precision-engineered pumps convert energy efficiently, but can be expensive to buy. However, their low running costs and the savings in electricity over a five-year period may make them worth the investment.

In a gravity-fed system, water is pumped from the filter to a waterfall, from where it flows back to the pond. The height of the waterfall plus the pressure loss in the pipes due to friction and bends adds up to a "head of water" against which the pump works. If the waterfall is too high for the pump's capacity, a lot of expensive energy will be used to produce a small trickle of water. To create a reasonable waterfall requires at least 66 gallons (250 L) of water per minute, depending on the width of the waterfall.

Pumps will rarely run for more than five years without needing replacement bearings, bushes, or shafts. Inquire about maintenance, spare parts, and the need for specialized tools before you make a final purchasing decision.

Mechanical filter

Filtration allows fecal matter, food particles, and airborne dust to precipitate and collect for easy removal from the system. In its simplest form, a filter is nothing more than an empty space (the settlement chamber) with a tapered bottom from which waste matter can be flushed.

Mechanical filters may take the form of a sedimentation bed or basin, a vortex or whirl separator, sand filters, and screens or rotating drums. Solids down to 40 microns will settle out by gravitational force, depending on how good the design is. Some filters can remove particulate matter as small as 20 microns (including larger microscopic parasites) but these are costly, with low flow rates. Systems with 200 micron screens are more common and practical. While some designs offer semi-automatic operation, all mechanical filters require accumulated waste matter to be removed regularly. The more effective filters are, the more maintenance they require to keep them operating smoothly.

Pumps and power

The work a pump can do is specified in terms of the flow rate that can be achieved at a specific pressure. Flow rates are expressed in gallons or liters per minute, cubic feet per hour, etc., while pressure is shown in pascals, bars, or meters of water (height).

The delivery capacity of a pump is related to its power consumption. As pumps run on electricity, a pump that is either too strong, or not strong enough, is wasteful and will impact negatively on your long-term running costs.

Study your utility bill to establish the monthly running cost of your pump. For example, a 450 watt pump running 24 hours a day will consume $0.45 \times 24 \times 30 = 324$ kWh (units) of electricity per month. Your utility bill should indicate the cost per unit and the total must be added to your budget.

When selecting a biological filter, choose a brand that is well supported by local repair or maintenance companies.

Biological filter

This is, effectively, an extension of the inner surface area of the pond. In a biological filter, large colonies of nitrifying bacteria grow inside the filter chamber, forming a layer of slime on the surface of a filter medium. These bacteria ultimately convert toxic ammonia into nontoxic nitrates. The filter medium must allow water to pass through with as little resistance as possible and should not clog easily.

Biological filters can be created with oyster shells, gravel, small bioballs, or anything else to which bacteria can easily attach. Filter media should not clog quickly, become soggy, or disintegrate over time. Avoid plastic shavings, foam, or sponge materials that have been treated with fire retardants, algicides, or germicides, as they could poison the fish.

Commercial biological filters come in different designs and at varying prices. Select the unit best suited for your pond size and carrying capacity and follow the manufacturer's instructions regarding pump size and maintenance. If you decide to build a biofilter, stick to accepted design principles and ensure that the filter media are easy to clean and maintain.

Undue emphasis is sometimes placed on the surface area of the filter medium while the importance of the water turnover rate through and over the filter is underrated. For example, if there are 24, 20-inch (50 cm) long koi in the pond, their total body mass will be 92 pounds (42 kg). If they are fed 35 percent protein food at 1.5 percent of total body mass, their daily food requirement will be 1.4 pounds (640 g). At water temperatures of 59–68°F (15–20°C), a filter surface area of 1,080 square feet (100 m²) will carry enough bacteria to convert the ammonia produced by the fish as a result of their daily diet.

UV treatment

Algae and bacteria, which proliferate during the first months of a new pond's life, can be controlled by ultraviolet (UV) treatment (sometimes referred to as UV sterilization). A clarifying unit will eliminate free-flowing algae and bacteria, allowing the natural beneficial flora of a pond to become established much faster. The bacterial count in koi ponds tends to be high because heterotrophic bacteria, which can be pathogenic, benefit from uneaten food and excrement in the pond. Reducing the bacterial count will reduce the possibility of opportunistic bacterial diseases.

UV treatment is cheap and effective if the recommended flow specification (the amount of water passing through the unit) is adhered to. Because their efficiency is controlled by the contact time, UV clarifiers should be fitted with a bypass control valve if there is any likelihood of the flow rate being too high because, if this is the case, only partial sterilization will take place. It is important to select the right unit for the size of your pond and remember to change the UV-light tubes every 9 to 12 months.

Ozonizers

The application of ozone is very effective for the removal of microbial organisms, organic compounds, and pesticides. Even nitrite, nitrate, proteins, and long-chain organic molecules that tend to form froth are oxidized by ozone, resulting in a significant reduction in the demand for biological oxygen. Ozone application must be precisely controlled. Improved, low-cost ozonization equipment is readily available and finding its way into some hi-tech koi ponds.

A UV unit will help to remove unwanted algae and bacteria from the pond.

A typical pond and filter design

An ideal pond system uses the natural flow of the water to collect solids and move them to the point where mechanical filtration can take place, followed by biological filtration and sterilization. The pump should be located at a point after filtration is completed, and must direct the flow through a waterfall or flow meter in order to aerate the water and provide movement (current) throughout the entire pond.

Bottom drains remove the solids and stale water to the filter system.

A natural vegetation filter should be raised above surface level (approx. 8-12 in./20-30 cm deep). Clean water from the filtration system can be returned to the pond via a waterfall.

A flow meter aerates water coming into the pond, thus improving the oxygen concentration.

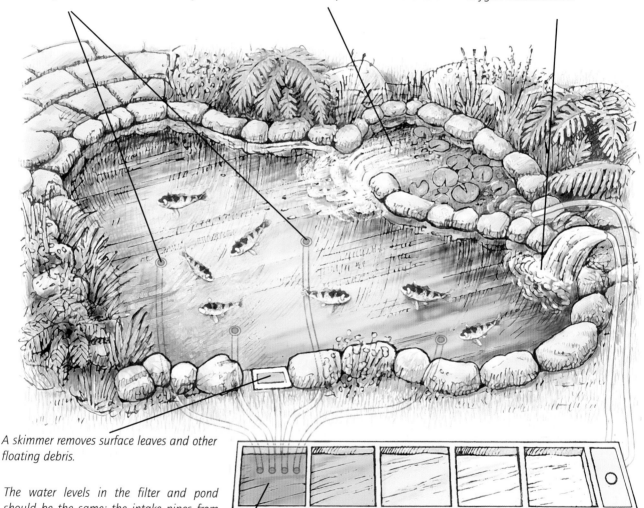

A skimmer removes surface leaves and other floating debris.

The water levels in the filter and pond should be the same; the intake pipes from the bottom drains run under the pond to the settlement chamber.

A settlement chamber allows the bulk of the solids and debris to settle out, after which they can be removed and disposed of in an environmentally responsible manner.

A series of biological filter chambers remove toxic ammonia and nitrites from the pond water. The chambers are normally covered to prevent debris entering the water.

The filtered water is pumped back into the pond via a waterfall, flow meter, or vegetable filter. A UV unit can be installed in the return path to treat the water and kill algae.

Good pond design always makes the best of the natural landscape. Here, a tree offers the koi shade from the summer sun.

Finishing and showing koi

What is beautiful and what is quality? While beauty is in the eye of the beholder, when it comes to determining quality in koi, koi-keepers have the advantage of set guidelines for body shape, color, pattern, and so on.

In your pond you will have some fish that are your favorites and others that are outstanding when compared with the rest of your collection. They can be appreciated for what they are, but how do they measure up against others? The only way to know is to enter them in a koi show where fish of the same variety and size compete—not against one another, but against the preferred standard of quality.

Evaluating koi

Koi are evaluated in terms of body shape, colors, pattern, and refinement. Without a good body, a koi will not show the elegant swimming style described as "beauty in motion." Add colors and patterns and this becomes "art in motion."

Luster, or finish, equates with refinement, but it is much more than just a high surface gloss. It is both that and the overall splendor of health and vitality that radiates from deep within an ideal koi.

When evaluating a koi, either for purchase or at a show, it is considered to be in poor taste, and demonstrates a lack of knowledge, to criticize the koi's weak points before praising its strong points. Whatever good or outstanding features a koi has must first be acknowledged, and the weaker points measured against those. Even a koi with obvious flaws may have some strong points.

Grading categories

Koi dealers sell fish according to grade and size, but standards are not universal, particularly outside Asia. What one dealer rates as top grade, another will label commercial grade.

In Japan, koi are grouped into four categories to describe their quality. *Yugoi* (excellent) is a koi that scores 80 percent for good qualities that by far outweigh any faults. *Ryogoi* (good) is when the fish has reasonably good looks, but faults and flaws account for up to 40 percent of the evaluation and cannot be redeemed by good points.

A koi with some strong points but no focal point, with faults and flaws amounting to 60 percent is *Bongoi* (average). If a fish has nothing but faults, it is *Dagoi* (poor).

Ideally, koi should not be appreciated only for the variety group to which they belong. However, at koi shows held in Asia, a *Kohaku*, *Sanke*, or *Showa* is generally selected as the Supreme Grand Champion; no other variety has won the top prize at a ZNA All-Japan Koi Show since the first show in 1969.

Koi shows are normally scheduled for the cooler months of the year when colors tend to be deeper and more even, the pattern more defined, and the fish flaunt their much-desired plump body shapes.

Finishing for shows

Koi need to be "finished" for a show. This means they must be polished for color, texture, and sheen, a process called *iro na shiagari*. During the warmer months, the koi will have gained growth but their colors and pattern might have dulled. Some koi might have gained in pattern, with markings emerging or submerging, while others will not have achieved any state of finish simply because their genetic make-up is programmed for later maturation.

Novice koi-keepers are frequently attracted to pretty, small fish with admirable finish—miniature versions of the great champion koi—as the appeal of instant beauty is greater than the appeal of eventual beauty. They purchase smaller fish in the belief that they will maintain their qualities, even improve on them, in the years to come. However, such koi have a high probability of losing their finish, their colors dulling, and the pattern breaking up as they mature. Ideally, small fish should be acquired on the basis of their potential to achieve quality when they grow bigger or reach adulthood.

Promoting growth and finish

To promote growth and finish, both the koi's feeding regime and the water quality in the pond must be exact. In their natural mud dam habitat, koi grub continuously and have the opportunity to develop good body shape through exercise in the pond's normally ample vertical and horizontal space. However, few koi-keepers have the opportunity to grow their fish in mud dams and so must maximize the characteristics of a concrete pond to emulate that of a mud dam.

A concrete pond should be twice as long as it is wide, with a minimum depth of 5 feet/1.5 m (see page 95). The total volume of water must have a filtration turnover rate of about one hour, but never more than three hours (see page 96), while the pumps and filter together must be capable of handling both the fish and the food load.

Consistently good water quality, stable water temperature, and fresh food with the correct amino acid and lipid make-up are other requirements that must be met with no or little compromise in order to achieve optimum finish in show fish.

Good food and water quality is essential for growth and finish in koi, particularly those with the potential to win awards.

Pretty fish are not necessarily show winners, so small fish should be acquired on the basis of their ability to improve.

Koi-keepers who are fortunate enough to have access to both mud dams and concrete ponds can manipulate the rate of growth and finish of their collections. The white ground of koi that have been reared in mud dams will show up as thick and cream-colored. By moving these koi into concrete ponds with high oxygen but low pH qualities, the white can be brightened over a period of a few weeks.

Mud ponds with "green" water have a high pH because of the presence of algae, which encourages good *hi* to develop and finish quickly. Therefore, koi that continue to show good *hi* after emerging from a mud dam are usually those whose *hi* was good in the first place. (Weak *hi* however, cannot be overcome or improved by putting the fish in "green" water.)

Melanin pigment is the base for *sumi* and can be promoted through a combination of the choice of food and the presence of minerals in a mud dam. The *sumi* of koi taken from a mud dam will usually be gray, dull, and submerged but will emerge, brighten, and gain luster within one or two weeks after being moved into clear water in a concrete pond.

Finishing a koi for a show is copying a natural process, but it demands time and skill. Koi-keepers who are impatient to see progress may succumb to the quick solution of overfeeding, particularly with color-enhancing food containing spirulina.

When finishing your koi, spirulina-enriched food should be introduced slowly and as part of the staple or wheat germ-based food. Too much color-enhancing food over too long a period will affect the quality of the white ground. Overfeeding can also promote a pot belly—not an attractive feature! Furthermore, fattening your koi will promote obesity which, in turn, may shorten their lifespan.

Better options for finishing are to increase the aeration in the pond, ensure a strong flow of water to exercise the fish, provide food that is easily and quickly digested, and limit the intake of color-enhancing food.

A strong, natural flow of water improves oxygenation and enables fish to exercise.

Showing koi

Local koi societies usually stage annual events that precede their national show. A local, or chapter, show is the ideal opportunity for novice koi-keepers to start showing, as it enables them to test the quality of their collection.

Smaller shows usually have fewer size groups, although the number is often determined by the budget and the available facilities at the venue.

In Japan, all the entries are generally grouped in specific ponds according to size and variety. Elsewhere, each participant is usually allocated one pool where all his or her entries are displayed, as this reduces the potential for the fish to transmit or catch viral or infectious diseases. (See page 108.)

Often, a fun class is incorporated to attract novice entrants, categories may include things like "the koi with the most appealing face" or "the koi with the most freckles."

Dealers and other koi specialists usually attend shows, and this is a golden opportunity to tap into a pool of knowledge and advice. It is also a chance for novices to gain first-hand experience of the camaraderie among koi-keepers.

Koi shows are usually advertised well in advance in the newsletters of koi societies and their local chapters. The notices will detail which varieties, or combinations of varieties, and size groups may enter.

Shows are usually either one- or two-day events. In the case of the latter, judging takes place on the first day and the awards ceremony on the second. Entries are accepted on the day preceding judging, and participating fish may only be removed at the conclusion of the show.

Koi enthusiasts study the entrants at a Japanese show. Portable ponds hold the various size categories.

Pre-show precautions

If possible, koi chosen for entry in a show should be kept in isolation for a week or so to observe them for any signs of injury and disease. This will eliminate the risk of your koi transmitting a disease or infection to other entries.

In countries where show organizers have reason to fear the spread of contagious diseases like KHV (Koi herpes virus), the English style of showing is adopted. Unlike the Japanese show format, where all the koi in a class are placed in a single vat or pool, in the English style, all entries are in individual pools to prevent any contact between competing koi from different owners. While this system protects the fish, it requires the judges to walk from pond to pond to adjudicate.

Another precaution to prevent, or at least limit, the spread of parasites and disease, is to ban fish from entering a show if they were imported within a period of four weeks, or taken from mud dams less than six weeks, prior to a show.

Feeding before a show

In the weeks preceding a show, feeding should be slowed down. During the last week, it should be stopped entirely. Koi that are "starved" in this way excrete less ammonia, consume less oxygen, and do not soil the water in the show ponds. It also makes the transition from the home pond to the show vat less stressful for the koi.

Pre-show preparations

One month before   Identify potential show fish, excluding any with obvious scars or fresh injuries. If possible, move the show entries to a pond with clear water so you can observe them on a daily basis. Start feeding wheat germ food, with the cautious addition of color enhancers, and commence treatment against parasites.

One week before   Cease all feeding. Confirm dates and times for entering and make sure you are aware of any show regulations. Arrange for helpers to assist with netting, bagging, and transporting the entries. Get in a supply of strong plastic bags to transport the fish and an oxygen cylinder for aerating the bags.

One day before   Check on the condition of your entries and make a final selection.

Show entry day   In the early morning, when it is still cool, net and bag the entries for transport to the show venue. You should have consulted in advance with the event organizer on the best time to arrive with your fish in order to avoid waiting in a line-up, particularly on a hot day. When you arrive, entry management teams will be on hand to assist you. Your fish, in their oxygenated bags, will be floated in waiting ponds while the administrative staff handle the paperwork, logging in your personal details, number of entries, and your payment, and allocate entry numbers to your fish. Handlers move the fish around in vats or bags. When it is your turn to de-bag your fish, each one will be inspected by a veterinarian or health expert. Diseased or severely stressed fish, or any with parasites or serious injuries will not be allowed to participate. Each fish will be identified according to its variety, measured, photographed, and allocated to the correct show pond. With such accurate identification, there is no chance that your fish can "get lost" among the other entries.

Show procedures

How a koi show is staged depends on the number of entries and the available show facilities, such as the number of vats in which to display the size groups (*bu*) of each variety.

For judging, size groups usually reflect stages of development. The smallest group could be 20 *bu* and these will be for fish of 8 inches (20 cm) and less in length, usually about six to nine months of age. Koi in the 25 *bu* class are entering their second year of age. The middle sizes are for three- to four-year-old koi, while bigger size classes accommodate koi reaching maturity and "adulthood."

On the day of judging, the show ponds are cordoned off to ensure privacy for the judges and freedom of access for the handlers who will be moving the fish around. After the judges have been introduced to the participants and the audience, they may commence judging either as a group or in teams, depending on how many entries there are. After the judging is completed, the awards ceremony will normally be presided over by the chairman of the local chapter or national society, as well as the officiating chief judge.

Once the official procedures have been concluded, the handling teams will assist with the debenching (removal of the fish from the show ponds). Each entrant must present a log of his or her entries as well as the photographs of all those fish, to ensure that the correct koi are returned to their owners. A receipt is signed as an acknowledgment of this.

An oxygen station will be made available by the organizers so that plastic bags can be aerated for the journey home.

There are some unwritten rules of etiquette at koi shows. Perhaps the most important is only to enter koi that do not have a major fault that would subject them to a penalty, as well as negate any other qualities the fish might have.

A keeper who enters all the koi in his or her collection will be regarded with disdain for not having the knowledge or courage to select the best for participation. At most, only three koi should be entered per variety and size group.

A frowned-upon practice is when entrants hold court at the show vats, loudly proclaiming how their fish surpass all the others. Discussions or comments should be dignified.

Show points system

The points system serves as a guideline, focusing attention on specific features. In the end, a koi with "beauty through balance" will be the winner because it has achieved quality in the sum of its shape, pattern, color, and overall elegance, without excessive loss of points for faults and flaws.

Body shape	50 points
Color	20 points
Pattern	10 points
Gracefulness	10 points
Dignity (character)	10 points

Show checklist

For the fish

- Sturdy, large new plastic bags
- An ample supply of strong rubber (elastic) bands
- Portable oxygen cylinder
- Crates, vats, or thick blankets in which to secure the bags for transportation to and from the show.
- Ice blocks or freezer packs to keep the bags cool
- Medication to treat the water in the bags

For yourself

- A set of dry clothes
- Rubber boots
- Raincoat and/or umbrella
- Sunscreen and hat (if the show is held outdoors)
- Camera
- Refreshments
- Money for entry fees

Becoming a judge

Many koi societies are members of the ZNA (Zen Nippon Airinkai), the leading organization for koi both within and outside Japan. Member societies have the right to request the ZNA to nominate one or more judges to adjudicate their shows.

The ZNA judges, who are drawn from around the world, have vast knowledge and experience in officiating and are widely respected. No judges have commercial interests to promote.

Along with the ZNA judges, the host society usually appoints trainee judges from within its own membership. The society also has the right to invite trainee judges from anywhere in the world; those favored in this way usually consider the invitation to be a singular honor.

The transition from trainee to local judge requires an unbroken five-year membership in the ZNA, to have officiated as a junior judge at several shows, attended ZNA judging seminars, and for your nomination to be recognized and approved by the ZNA. Many more years of judging are required to become a certified ZNA judge, allowed to officiate internationally.

Koi dealers and professional koi breeders can qualify for judge status via Shinkokai (the All-Japan Nishikigoi Association), but only in exceptional cases are they invited to adjudicate at ZNA shows.

The first step toward becoming a fully fledged judge is to study koi closely at all opportunities.

Judging criteria

Body shape, color, and pattern are judged in that order. The body shape takes priority because, irrespective of the standard of color and pattern, a body that is too long, too short, too thin, or too round will constitute inferior quality. The bigger and better the body shape, the better the impression; and the better a koi's movement will be. A koi with a pot belly cannot have a graceful swimming motion. Deformities demand immediate elimination (although it is questionable whether the koi should have been entered at all).

Faults and flaws are tolerated according to the degree of severity. For example, the complete absence of barbels is a serious fault, whereas missing barbels is a flaw. Blindness in one eye or a missing eye is a fault but an eye showing a white or red film is a flaw. A head that is too round, too square, or has a "pinched" look will detract from the koi's appeal.

Fins must be in proportion to the body, not too large, too small, too square, or too rounded. It is considered a fault if the fins of small and medium-size koi are too long or short, while similar fins on large koi will usually eliminate them from top rankings. The absence of a significant part or a whole fin is a fault; healed or partial damage is a flaw.

In evaluating color, judges will search for an even hue without weakness or fading. The white ground must be pure and thick, the *hi* and *sumi* must have depth and brightness, and metallic ground colors must be even, without any smudging. The sought-after luster of the skin can be visualized as a thin layer of high-gloss varnish.

Judges are especially attentive of *kiwa* (see page 39) that is sharp and attractive. The pattern should be typical of the variety and balanced along the length of the body. In smaller koi, the pattern should be appealing. Young koi should show elegant, refined patterns, while adult koi must have splendor and presence. Two further criteria used in judging are gracefulness and character; and here subjective preferences come into play. Gracefulness can be equated with elegance, tidiness, and refinement; character is the overall impression, the undeniable presence of a superlative synthesis of all the koi's features.

Traditionally, judging starts with the jumbo and bigger size *bu* from which a Jumbo Champion, Reserve Grand Champion, and Supreme Grand Champion (overall winner) are selected.

The judges then go to the smallest *bu* and work their way up to the biggest *bu* to find first, second, and third places from each variety. From among all the winners in a specific *bu*, a Supreme Champion for that size group is selected, and the process is repeated for all the other *bu*.

With all the Supreme Champions in separate ponds, the judges vote for a Junior Grand Champion and Baby Grand Champion from amongst the smaller *bu*. The judges may be asked to select a single koi in each *bu* that they would rate a *tategoi* (a young fish with the potential to achieve excellence as it matures).

The chief judge has the right to overrule any decision, even if the judges and trainee judges have made a choice by ballot. The relatively short history of koi-keeping in the West is no excuse for not aspiring toward quality. Judges should not adjust their criteria to compensate for lack of quality. It is not a case of judging the best of what is available, but of measuring entrants against the standard. Therefore, should the judges decide to withhold an award, their decision must always be accepted and respected.

A very large koi receives careful handling from show staff.

Post-show treatments

Option A Transport the koi in oxygenated bags of roughly 10–15 gallon capacity (38–56 L) filled with about 3 gallons (11 L) of water to which 2 teaspoons (10 ml) of a 0.2 percent potassium permanganate stock solution has been administered (made up at a ratio of 2 g per L). Pack no more than 8–10 pounds (4–5 kg) of fish per bag.

On your return home, isolate the koi in a quarantine tank at above 65°F (18°C) for seven to ten days. Check the fish daily and administer antiparasitic treatment (see page 138) at the first sign of stress or disease. If you can make a proper diagnosis of any problem, treat accordingly. Ensure optimum water quality in the quarantine tank and avoid cross-contamination with the main pond until the quarantine period is over. (This is the recommended option.)

Option B Transport as per Option A. On your return home, release the koi into the pond, to which has been added 11 pounds (5 kg) of coarse salt per 264 gallons (1,000 L) of water. (Ideally, koi should be placed in a quarantine tank, but if you don't have one, this is a workable alternative.)

Making an oxygenated bag

Place the koi, together with an appropriate amount of pond water (about one-third of the bag's volume), into a sturdy plastic bag, or even a double bag (top and center right).

Using a properly metered oxygen cylinder (available from medical supply companies or hardware stores), inflate the bag (bottom right) before sealing it with a rubber band and placing it in a suitable container for transportation to the show.

Transporting koi

When fish are transported over long distances, the water they travel in can become very acidic due to the carbon dioxide that they exhale during the journey.

A typical load of 9 pounds (4 kg) of koi placed in a plastic bag for transport would require 16 gallons (60 L) of oxygen over a 24-hour period. However, when koi are starved of food for three or more days, their gut is not only cleared, but their oxygen consumption is reduced to as little as 20 percent of the normal requirement. The same fish will now require less than about 3½ gallons (13 L) of oxygen, making even intercontinental air travel possible. Koi that are transported from Japan are always starved beforehand to avoid any risk of stress induced by oxygen shortage. As soon as they arrive at their destination, it is important to get the fish into fresh, oxygenated water as soon as possible.

When moving fish over short distances, such as to and from local shows, it is not necessary to starve them beforehand (although fish are usually starved before being entered into a show, see page 108). The standard practice is to fill a large plastic bag with about one-third water and two-thirds oxygen, making sure that larger fish have enough water in the bag to stay upright and that their gills are covered.

If your journey is less than one hour, the fish will survive in a bag filled with normal air.

Post-show practice

At the end of a show there is usually a rush to net, bag, and prepare koi for the return journey to their home ponds. If the process is not handled with care, fish may become stressed and could even become injured.

On returning home from a show, regardless of whether or not the koi are in good condition, it is advisable to keep them in isolation for up to two weeks (see opposite). Feed them lightly with wheat germ–based food and scrutinize them daily for injuries or symptoms of disease, treating anything promptly.

Bruises or small cuts can be treated at home with antibiotics, but anything more serious, such as deep cuts or torn fins, needs professional attention, particularly if stitches are required (see Chapter 8, Health care).

In the Japanese method of showing, all the entries in a single class are presented in the same pond, where they can be examined by the judges in a single viewing.

Feeding

The secret for achieving good growth, striking color, and optimum health over a koi's lifetime is to provide the fish with a sustained supply of quality nutrition (food) as well as variety in its diet.

If a koi's nutrition is poor in its developmental stages, there is simply no way in later years for the fish to catch up or repair the damage, and it will remain stunted and underdeveloped, regardless of the quality of its environment.

In their natural state, all carp are omnivorous, with a bottom-foraging feeding habit. They consume small amounts of food continually throughout the day, sucking and chewing their food, while feeding off both the surface and the bottom.

Koi that are returned to mud dams soon revert to the natural feeding pattern of carp, and are often referred to as the "pigs" of the fish world because of their ability to consume virtually any food source, from fresh or rotting plant matter to insects, worms, and other small water organisms.

A koi's ability to thrive on a large variety of food substances has great advantages for the hobbyist. As koi do not have a stomach, they will feed almost continuously if given the opportunity. At moderate temperatures (64-77°F/18-25°C) a healthy koi ought to consume between one and three percent of its body weight in food each day, depending on the temperature and the frequency of feeding.

Carp are known to achieve their best growth rate when they are fed 6.5 percent of their body mass per day, in nine equal portions, at a water temperature of 73°F (23°C). However, this feeding regime is neither practical nor prudent for most koi enthusiasts; not only will the cost be exorbitant, but the pond will be under stress to cope with the increased demand for oxygen and the removal of excreted waste.

The average water temperature dictates the rate at which koi digest and absorb food. Digestion slows down considerably in cooler water, so feeding must be decreased, or even halted, during the winter months.

Avoid heavy feeding when the water temperature is above 77°F (25°C). Digestion requires oxygen and, as warm water holds less dissolved oxygen than cooler water, sufficient oxygen cannot be supplied for efficient digestion to take place. At a water temperature of 68°F (20°C) digestion takes four to five

Regular feeding with the correct type and quantity of food will help your koi to grow to their maximum potential.

hours. The passage of food through the gut slows as water temperature decreases and, at 41°F (5°C), all feeding will cease. For best growth and utilization of their feed, the water temperature should range between 73°F and 86°F (23°C and 30°C), although higher levels should not be maintained for long periods, to avoid excessively fast metabolic rates.

Unlike free-living carp, pond-raised koi are dependent on when and what their keeper provides. Koi kept in an artificial environment should be given a varied diet that includes as many live organisms as possible, thereby copying nature so that the nutrients promote cell growth, provide energy, and sustain organ function. The result should be a healthy koi with a plump (but not fat) body shape and bright colors.

Health, growth, and reproductive ability are directly related to the proteins, fats, carbohydrates, vitamins, and minerals that koi consume, and koi-keepers should have a basic but sound understanding of the quality, ideal quantity, and effect of each of these dietary elements.

An important aspect of koi nutrition, which is commonly ignored by feed manufacturers, are the intestinal bacteria that assist with digestion and provide supplemental nutrients (in effect, enabling koi to thrive for periods on an unbalanced diet). Intestinal bacteria can be affected by disease and medication but are replenished naturally after illness.

Protein

Proteins contain amino acids (the basic building blocks of all living cells), which are required in large quantities for tissue synthesis during growth and cell replacement. Adult koi have a dietary protein requirement of 28–35 percent of their body weight, with a metabolizable energy of about 3.6 kilocalorie/gram (15 kilojoules/g). For young, growing fish, a feed with 35–45 percent protein content is recommended.

Koi require 10 essential amino acids to ensure good heath and normal growth. These are arginine, histidine, isoleucine, leucine, lysine, methionine, phenylalanine, threonine, tryptophan, and valine. Deficiencies in any one of these amino acids can lead to growth retardation, skeletal deformities, and any

of a range of systemic disease syndromes and growth disorders. Studies done on the demand for various amino acids indicate that koi not only require high levels of protein in their diet, but also need animal or bacterial protein for optimal growth. Plant proteins alone are not sufficient to supply all these requirements, so koi can never be true vegetarians.

Fish meal, soya meal, and corn germ contain most of the 10 essential amino acids in the right quantities and make up the bulk of the protein in most commercial koi feeds.

Live earthworms, bloodworms, mealworms, silkworm pupae, and insects, both alive or preserved, are rich in protein and other nutrients and are considered by koi as delicacies. Raw ox heart or liver cut in strips can be a good replacement for earthworms, both in sight and in nutritional value, but other meat should be avoided because of its high fat content. Frozen shrimp will be consumed with vigor.

Pond-raised koi depend completely on food being provided for them on a regular basis.

Lipids (fats)

Lipids, or fats, comprise chains of fatty acids bonded together with molecules of glycerol. They provide energy and are essential for tissue synthesis, in particular cell wall construction. Koi have a great need for unsaturated fatty acids, so feed should have a minimum content of 8 percent lipids.

Consumed in excess, lipids can cause obesity in koi, but a diet that is lipid-deficient will result in fin erosion and heart and liver problems.

In commercial feeds, fish meal, soya, corn oils, and wheat germ are the best sources of lipids. Earthworms, silkworm pupae, and other insects are natural lipid-containing foods and are also rich in essential fatty acids.

Carbohydrates

Carbohydrates (starches) are the digestible medium in which commercially derived nutrition is delivered to the gut of the fish. A typical koi diet can contain up to 30–35 percent carbohydrates, with wheat starch, extracted from cereal, being the most easily metabolized. Because koi metabolize carbohydrates less readily than lipids, they are the secondary source of energy in the diet.

In commercially produced koi foods, the carbohydrate is cooked during the process of pelletizing or extrusion, which greatly improves its digestibility.

Some carbohydrates are converted into muscular and abdominal fat. An excess of carbohydrate in a diet may result in the degeneration of the hepatopancreas function, as fat cells displace and suppress the activity of liver and pancreatic cells. Liver and heart failure is usually the end-result of obesity in koi.

Koi should be fed both protein and vegetable matter. Bloodworms (top right) are a good source of nutrients. The larvae of brine shrimp (nauplii) (right) can be fed to fry during their first days, but after that it is less costly to feed them on algae, boiled egg yolk, and daphnia. They should get flake or paste feed from about half an inch (1 cm) and floating dry pellets from about 1 inch (2.5 cm) into adulthood.

VITAMINS: FUNCTIONS, SOURCES, AND RESULTS OF DEFICIENCIES

VITAMIN	FUNCTION/BENEFITS	SOURCES	RESULTS OF A DEFICIENCY
A	Healthy skin Eyesight	Fish liver oils, liver, carrots, green and yellow vegetables	Anorexia, fading color, hemorrhages of the skin and kidney, poor growth, blindness
B1	Nerve function Digestion Reproduction	Meat, dried yeast, whole-wheat, bran, oatmeal, vegetables	Poor growth, fading color, fin paralysis, hemorrhaging at fin bases
B2	Aids growth; helps carbohydrate metabolism and oxygen absorption in muscle and tissue	Liver and kidney, yeast, green leafy vegetables	Retarded growth, anemia, loss of appetite, bleeding in the eyes or from the gills and nostrils
B6	Aids the metabolism of protein; contributes to blood formation	Meat, wheat, yeast, green vegetables	Poor appetite, ataxia, nervous disorders, epileptic fits, abdominal dropsy, rapid ventilation of the gills, pop-eye disease
B12	Promotes growth, increases energy, forms and regulates red blood cells	Meat and yeast	Anemia
C	Combats viral and bacterial infections, heals wounds, plays a role in the development of cartilage and collagen	Green and leafy vegetables	Deformities of the spine and gills, internal hemorrhaging, lack of resistance to infection
E	An important antioxidant (preventing fat from turning rancid)	Wheat germ, vegetable oils, leafy vegetables, and whole-grain cereals	Anemia, clubbed gills, exopthalmia, skeletal disorders, fatty degeneration of the liver, declining reproduction, poor growth
Nicotinic acid	Crucial to promote growth in young koi	Meat	Anorexia, anemia, muscle spasms, swollen gills, skin hemorrhage, lethargy
Choline	Contributes to the utilization of fats and cholesterol	Meat, cereal, and wheat germ	Anemia, fatty liver degeneration, hemorrhage in kidneys and intestines
Pantothenic acid	Important in the process of metabolizing fat and carbohydrates	Liver and kidney	Loss of appetite, abnormal mucus production, flared opercula, necrosis of the jaw, barbels, and fins
Folic acid	Contributes to red blood cell and tissue cell formation	Liver, kidney, yeast, deep-green leafy plants	Anemia, anorexia, exopthalmia, lethargy, pale gills, poor growth

Vitamins

Vitamins represent chemical compounds that are essential for the normal functioning of the koi's internal organs, but which it cannot synthesize by itself. Vitamins are needed in regular small quantities, but a vitamin-deficient diet will lead to serious developmental, growth, and general health problems.

In nature, koi source vitamins from whole, raw organisms, such as worms and insects, as well as from plants and algae. Even rotten plant matter can be a source of some vitamins. The vitamin content of a koi's diet can be increased by offering fresh vegetables like whole lettuce, squashed green peas, and diced carrots.

A premix of vitamins is normally added to commercial feeds to cater for the full range of essential vitamins needed by koi. Some vitamins degenerate with age while others, notably Vitamin C, are sensitive to heat. Feed manufacturers are aware of this and normally compensate for the loss of vitamins during the cooking process. However, the long shelf life of some feeds can lead to a loss of nutrient value over time.

Better quality koi foods have higher levels of vitamins C and E than required, as both have major health benefits and function as antioxidants to prevent lipids turning rancid.

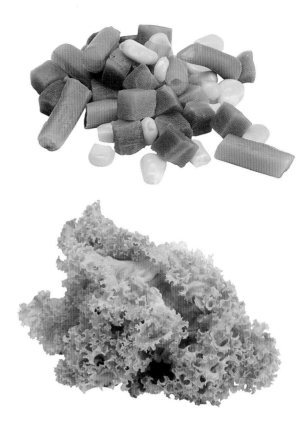

Add essential vitamins by including a variety of diced fresh vegetables (top) or lettuce (above) in your koi's menu.

Minerals

Minerals are inorganic chemicals required by fish for various metabolic functions, as well as to build skeletal structures and nerves, and support the efficient exchange of gases in the blood system; they are also an active component in the osmo-regulation process.

Calcium, magnesium, phosphorus, copper, iron, manganese, zinc, iodine, and selenium are considered essential minerals. The source of these is the ash component of commercial koi food, which averages around 12 percent. Koi also obtain minerals from their environment, as trace amounts are found in sufficient quantity in water for absorption via their gills.

Bone deformities, loss of muscle tone, loss of appetite, obesity, anemia, and skin problems are all typical symptoms of a mineral deficiency.

Commercially produced pellets, containing mainly fish meal, are an easy and convenient way to feed, allowing accurate measurement and minimal waste.

Moisture

All commercial ("dry") koi foods contain a certain percentage of moisture, which comes from both the manufacturing and the cooking processes. After extrusion, the pellets are dried to below 10 percent moisture.

It is absolutely vital that commercial foods are stored in a dry place. If the food gets damp, the yeast will cause the carbohydrates to ferment, while fungi find the rich substrate an ideal growth medium. Certain fungi that grow on the corn and alfalfa components of feed can be severely toxic to fish, so never give moldy feed to your fish.

Color enhancers

During the growth season, a koi's colors are subdued, only deepening when the water cools down. During this time, feed should not include color enhancers, as these accelerate the development of pigment cells, which deteriorate once maturity is achieved. Restrict color-enhancing food to the cool months and even then use it sparingly and as a supplement.

The preferred color enhancer is spirulina, an algae, which fixes and promotes the *hi*. It must be given sparingly, and at the right time of the year, as overfeeding with spirulina can cause a yellowing of the white color. Spirulina cannot "cure" genetically poor-quality color.

Commercial color-enhancing feeds may contain other natural sources of color pigments, like shrimp, crab, lobster, flower petals, corn, alfalfa, paprika, yeast species like *Phaffia rhodozoma*, and microalgae like *Haematococcus pluvialis*. Synthetically produced pigments are identical in chemical structure, although they are more concentrated and stable, improving both the control of the pigment mix and the quality of the end product.

Carotenoids are fat-soluble pigments produced by plants, algae, and plankton. Higher animals cannot produce them and have to consume small amounts in their diet in order for them to be deposited in their pigment cells. The red coloring in koi pigment cells comes from astaxanthin and canthaxanthin while the yellow comes from lutein and zeaxanthin.

Natural color enhancers found in certain foodstuffs can help to bring out the best in your koi.

Food options

For optimum health, koi should be fed on commercial koi food or a mixture of commercial food and fresh or frozen items.

The typical food formulation is 35-40 percent protein, 8 percent lipids, 30-35 percent carbohydrates, 1-3 percent vitamins, and 12 percent ash (minerals). The remainder, typically 8-10 percent, is taken up by moisture.

Sources of the these ingredients include fish meal, wheat, soybean meal, crab meal, yellow corn, brewer's yeast, and whole egg. Avoid feed containing meat or bone meal because it reduces palatability, especially for younger fish.

Floating pellets encourage the koi to come to the surface to feed, bringing them close for inspection. Uneaten food can also be scooped up, reducing debris in the water, but sinking pellets are usually much cheaper. Neither type should disintegrate too quickly and both should have sufficient binding ingredients to prevent the leaching of water-soluble nutrients.

Bear in mind that koi are natural bottom feeders whose mouthparts have evolved for eating from the pond floor. Although hungry koi will scour the bottom between feeds, leftover food should be removed after a suitable interval.

Top brand-name commercial koi foods will satisfy all nutritional requirements, as well as meeting the required standards of quality. Vacuum-packed or freeze-dried food has a long shelf life, ensuring freshness, with less chance of the lipids going rancid or the proteins and vitamins degenerating. On the other hand, paste food has the advantage of easy digestion and greater stability of the nutrients.

In addition to packaged foods, fresh items, such as earthworms, shrimp, bloodworms, garden snails, lettuce leaves, or even boiled rice can be fed. Avoid white bread, as it contains a mild form of bleach.

Raw beans, peas, and corn kernels have hard outer casings that koi cannot digest, but they can be a valuable food resource if cooked and mashed before feeding.

Quantity

It is as important to feed the right amount of food as to feed the right type of food. A diet too high in carbohydrates, lipids, or protein will produce obese koi. Overfed koi produce too much ammonia, and the added burden placed on the biofilter can lead to a deterioration in water quality.

With patience, you can get your koi to eat from your hand, bringing them close enough to inspect their condition.

A safe guide is to feed only as much as the koi will eat in five minutes. You can feed small quantities as often as you like—one to three times a day is the norm—but all uneaten food should be removed after five minutes. Food that is not eaten will decay, leading to increased levels of ammonia, phosphates, and other organic compounds, and attracting potentially harmful bacteria and fungi.

Freshness

Store your koi food in a sealed container in a cool place, as exposure to the atmosphere for any length of time can cause a deterioration in quality. Feed that is older than six or eight months, and which has been exposed to air, will have lost much of its nutritional value, causing the proteins and vitamins to become unstable and degenerate.

If you purchase large quantities of koi food, repackage it into smaller quantities in resealable plastic bags and store these in a refrigerator or a cool place.

Most commercial koi feeds provide a balanced meal, having been formulated especially to meet the requirements of koi in an artificial environment. Check the packaging for information on recommended portion sizes, to ensure you don't feed more than your koi can eat in a limited period.

Feeding programs

How much and when to feed is dictated by the size of the koi and the seasonal conditions. In warmer water, there is a greater need for growth and energy, which is provided in many commercial feeds, as well as staple (basic) food. In cooler water, koi require the easily digestible nutrients found in wheat germ, rice, and vegetable protein.

At the start of spring, as koi begin to emerge from their state of near-hibernation, their digestive system has to be activated by feeding small quantities of easily digestible wheat germ-based food. During summer, koi need quality sources of growth and energy food that comes from staple food with its adequate quantities of protein and lipids. Staple food must be fed in small quantities, several times per day.

In the fall, as growth slows down, the koi color up and their patterns become more defined. At the start of the season, give a mixture of staple food and wheat germ, offering mainly wheat germ as the water cools down.

When the water temperature falls below 50°F (10°C) in winter, all feeding can be suspended, provided the koi are in good condition, with adequate body fat. Feeding can be resumed when the water temperature stabilizes above 50°F (10°C). Healthy koi will easily survive the winter on their reserves of body fat.

Commercial pellets should be stored in airtight containers to keep out moisture, which will cause spoilage.

Health care

Disease is a disruption of the normal functions and processes of any living organism. Koi with a healthy, normally functioning immune system are generally able to live and thrive in the presence of pathogens. However, under adverse environmental conditions, they can become stressed. Stress triggers a hormonal change that, ultimately, has a negative impact on the immune system and the fish's ability to fight disease.

When fish are kept in high densities, it is easy for disease to proliferate, particularly if basic living conditions are not met. All koi-keepers need a working knowledge of koi health care to enable them to recognize and treat diseases and minor ailments.

Diseases are the result of interaction between a host, a pathogen (a disease-causing agent, like a bacteria, parasite, or virus), and the environment. Diseases in koi can be infectious or noninfectious. Infectious diseases are caused by micro-organisms that challenge the fish's defense mechanisms by invading, infecting, and disrupting the normal functioning of the host. Noninfectious diseases are caused by factors such as environmental conditions, nutritional deficiencies, or toxins.

Because fish are cold-blooded animals, their entire metabolism, and therefore their response to infection, depends on the water temperature. The activities of many pathogens present in the pond environment are also linked to water temperature and, consequently, there is no fixed incubation period for the onset of most infectious diseases. This impacts on the effective quarantining period when screening new fish for disease.

If your pond water temperature may drop to below 50°F (10°C) in winter, consult your local aquatic store and koi club for information on how to best overwinter your koi.

Environmental health factors

A healthy koi collection can almost be guaranteed, provided pond water meets the minimum requirements of dissolved oxygen (see page 76), and toxicity levels are not exceeded. If these factors drift beyond the optimum limits, the fish are put under stress. If adverse conditions persist, gill tissue or internal organs will be affected, resulting in secondary infection or death. Long-term exposure to poor-quality water has a negative effect on the way a fish responds to physiological stress.

Stress response

When a fish senses a potentially harmful situation, an alarm response is triggered. Whether it is the sight of a predator or the detection of a toxic substance in the water, the initial physiological changes are the same: hormones are released to increase the heart rate and blood pressure, and cause a rise in blood sugar and lactic acid levels. These changes occur in an instant and prepare the fish for a "fight or flight" response to the perceived stress. In the short term, the fish will suffer no ill effects and the metabolism returns to normal once the stress factor is removed.

If the stress persists, however, the fish will adapt to the adverse conditions but will, in effect, live a stressful existence. Permanent physiological changes will result in an immune-suppressed state, making the fish susceptible to disease. Other consequences are a poor appetite, reduced growth rate, and interference with the reproductive processes.

Fish that have been in an immune-suppressed state for an extended period cannot withstand environmental shock, such as sudden temperature or pH changes, and will easily succumb to parasitic or bacterial infections.

The eventual outcome of severe and prolonged stress is exhaustion. A fish in this state can seldom be rescued and death usually follows. However, in the spirit of the hobby, some koi-keepers take up the challenge and through sensible health management, which may include a regime of force-feeding, antibiotics, and antiparasitic treatments, may nurse an ailing fish back to health and vitality.

Waterfalls flowing swiftly not only aerate the water, but aid in the degasing of noxious gases and the removal of organic pollutants. In addition, waterfalls enhance the esthetic beauty of a pond.

The importance of water quality

The artificial environment of the pond is frequently the source of chronic stress and secondary infections in koi. If a koi collection is prone to disease, the source of the problem must be found before the disease can be successfully treated.

Maintaining optimum water quality is an important factor in reducing disease. Seasonal temperature changes can exacerbate the appearance of fungal diseases like *Branchiomyces* (gill rot), or lead to outbreaks of parasites such as *Ergasilus* (gill maggot), *Ichthyophirius* (white spot), *Argulus* (fish louse), and *Lernaea* (anchor worm), although the latter two should not be present in a well-managed pond.

Gas supersaturation

Gill infections and ulcers can be indirectly caused by gas supersaturation, which occurs when the pressure drops or the temperature of the inflowing water increases significantly.

Dissolved gases, mainly nitrogen, cause small bubbles (gas emboli) to form in the blood vessels of the gills and skin. These bubbles block the flow of blood, damaging surrounding tissue and causing secondary infections when the tissue dies.

Pond surface water may become supersaturated with oxygen during the day due to photosynthesis by green plants. (This is the process by which plants use energy from the sun to produce food molecules, in the form of carbohydrates, from carbon dioxide and water.)

While fish can tolerate oxygen saturation, chronic gas supersaturation due to nitrogen build-up is cause for concern. This rare event can be caused by leaky pump intake connections that "crush" air into the water as it is returned to the pond. (If bubbles form on the hairs on the back of your hand when you submerge it, your pond may have a gas embolism problem.) To prevent air being sucked in, especially if sand filters are used, intake lines to high-pressure pumps should be assembled using rigid pipes that have glued and screw-in fittings.

Water from deep wells may be supersaturated with nitrogen and low in oxygen so, as a precaution, it should be vigorously aerated before use in koi ponds.

Behavioral symptoms

Spend time studying your koi, as deviations from normal appearance or behavior could indicate a problem with their state of health. Visual observation is best done at feeding time when the fish rise to the surface and can be inspected from close up. Recognizable behavioral changes normally precede visible signs of disease by a day or two, so quick action can save a sick koi, or even an entire collection.

Appetite

Any loss of appetite should be treated as an early warning sign for disease or stress. Low levels of dissolved oxygen, or high levels of carbon dioxide, ammonia, or nitrite in the water will immediately result in a poor response to food or even a complete refusal to eat.

Water temperatures above or below the preferred upper and lower limits (see page 73) will also result in reduced appetite, but in this case, the only response should be to feed less.

Activity levels

The three levels of abnormal activity are hyperactivity, sluggish or lethargic behavior, and a fish that appears comatose (not moving at all). Any changes in activity levels should be investigated to determine the cause.

Hyperactivity is a flight response, when the fish tries to escape something that it finds stressful and wants to avoid. It is characterized by rapid swimming, usually in a group, in circles around the periphery of the pond. Fish that are put into water with too-low pH or too-high levels of chlorine, ammonia, or other toxic compounds tend to be hyperactive in an effort to escape the toxins. A sudden rise in water temperature may also induce hyperactive behavior.

Sluggish or lethargic behavior is a sure sign of disease. Individual fish should be checked for parasites. Such behavior could also be due to exhaustion following a period of hyperactivity, or to a sudden cold or hot spell. The latter is often followed by a parasitic proliferation and infestation.

The best time to observe your koi is at feeding time, when they come to the surface. Spending time getting to know each fish's habits, movements, and appearance can often alert you to potential health problems before they get out of hand.

Comatose behavior is most likely due to an increased concentration of carbon dioxide in the blood, but low levels of oxygen, impaired gill function, or internal diseases can also give rise to this near-death state, as can a sudden drop in temperature or very cold conditions.

Body color

A reddening of the fins and belly due to capillary veins becoming visible indicates high blood pressure and a fish suffering from stress, most probably due to disease. Dull or gray skin can be due to a parasitic infestation.

Respiratory activity

Increased opercular (gill) movement is normally caused by a low concentration of dissolved oxygen, extremely hot conditions, ammonia, or nitrite poisoning. Gill damage due to toxic chemicals, bacteria, or parasites also causes rapid respiration. Decreased respiratory rate can be due to very cold conditions.

Swimming behavior

Hanging at the surface and gulping for air could be a symptom of gill damage caused by bacteria, parasites, or toxic chemicals, or be due to low levels of dissolved oxygen, or to extremely hot weather. Uncontrolled and uncoordinated swimming can result from an infection affecting the central nervous system, neurological damage from a stroke, or even organophosphate poisoning.

An infection of the swim bladder, or its filling with fluid, can cause the fish to sink slowly to the bottom of the pond, followed by fits of frantic swimming to gain height, especially when trying to eat.

Shyness

If a single fish hides away or stays separate from the group, it could be sick. If all the fish suddenly become skittish and hide when the pond is approached, they have probably been frightened by a predator that has awakened their "genetic memory" when attempting a strike. Be on the lookout for early morning visits from predatory birds.

Predatory birds, such as this heron, can create a sense of panic and stress when they wait at the side of the pond.

A lone fish circling the pond is usually either sick or stressed and should be netted for a closer inspection.

Anchor worms can be gently removed with tweezers. It is best to isolate the fish until it it is clear of the parasites.

A camera mounted on a microscope makes it possible to record images of parasites for later identification, or for reference.

Parasites

Under normal conditions, all fish carry parasites but are not affected by them. Internal parasites (endoparasites) live in the organs and blood while external, or ectoparasites, live on the skin, fins, and gills. In the case of a suspected invasion by parasites, fish lice, or leeches, the culprit should be identified swiftly with the aid of a microscope, and the correct treatment given immediately. Delaying treatment will increase the fish's misery and increase the mortality rate.

Repeatedly rubbing the flanks against pond edges or other objects (termed "flashing") can be an indication of external parasites irritating the fish. Parasitic infestations usually cause secondary bacterial and fungal diseases by breaking through the protective layers of the cuticle, exposing the tissue below and allowing opportunistic bacteria to enter. While parasites are relatively easy to identify and eradicate, bacteria and fungal diseases are more difficult to cure and may leave permanent lesions. Bacterial diseases may also be infectious.

Parasites can be easy to control with the correct chemical treatment but, to fully eradicate them, the cause of the infestation should be identified. Poor water conditions, sharp temperature changes, and newly introduced fish are usually to blame, so cure the pond and you will cure the fish.

Protozoan parasites

Normally, the only visible signs are clusters of single-celled, microscopic organisms on the skin or a general deterioration in skin condition. Common protozoan parasites are ich (*Ichthyophthirius*), *Trichodina*, *Costia* (*Ichthyobodo necator*), *Chilodonella*, *Glossatella*, and *Epistylis*. They have whip-like flagella or hair-like cilia to facilitate movement, and can only be accurately identified by examining a mucus scraping under a microscope. Immediate treatment with the correct medication usually ensures eradication and rapidly restores the fish to good health. Typical treatments are potassium permanganate, malachite green, and formalin.

Monogenetic trematodes or flukes

Flukes are a small external parasitic flatworm of which two types are a major cause of concern to koi-keepers. Gill flukes (*Dactylogyrus*) infect the gills and gill arches while body flukes (*Gyrodactylus*) are more likely to be found in the skin mucus. Once attached to the fish, flukes feed on the skin and gill tissue, causing function loss and secondary bacterial infection.

Flukes can only be correctly identified by examining a mucus scraping under a microscope. Typical treatments are potassium permanganate and praziquantel.

Parasitic crustaceans

Fish lice (*Argulus*), anchor worm (*Lernaea*), and gill maggots (*Ergasilus*) are ectoparasites visible to the naked eye that can cause severe damage to skin, scales, and gills if not controlled. Once introduced into a pond, the crowded conditions favor the chances of the free-living larval stages finding a host, causing a problem that will not resolve itself.

These parasites must be physically removed with tweezers from the affected fish and further treatments will be required to remove future generations of the parasites and ensure complete eradication. Your veterinarian may be able to recommend an appropriate treatment, and you should also consult your local koi club and aquatic store.

Ich, or white spot (Ichthyophthirius), *is a common protozoan parasite that occurs on the skin. The small white spots are clearly visible on the head of this fish.*

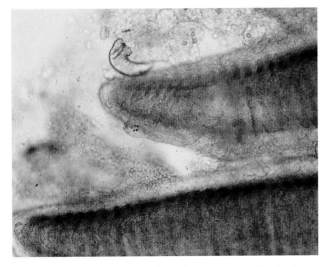

Gill flukes are external parasites of the flatworm family. They feed on the tissue, causing loss of function.

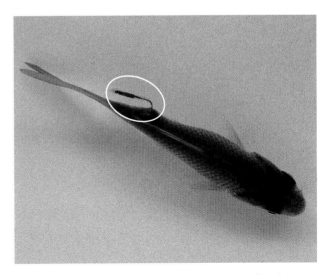

Anchor worm (shown in circle) *is an ectoparasite that can cause damage to the skin or scales if not controlled.*

Bacterial diseases

Most bacterial infections occur when the fish is in an immune-depressed state due to stress, or when the bacterial load in a pond overwhelms the fish's natural defenses.

Bacterial gill disease, fin rot, and tail rot are common names given to various diseases caused by *Flexibacter columnaris*, an

Fin rot and other bacterial diseases are caused by Flexibacter columnaris. *It can occur when the water quality is poor.*

An ulcer caused by Flavobacterium. *All ulcers must be treated immediately (*see page 136*) to avoid the infection spreading to other fish.*

organism that primarily affects the gill tissue, leading to fusion of the lamellae (see page 27). It occurs mostly at water temperatures above 59°F (15°C), when the water quality is poor. Lesions may be found on the gills, fins, mouth, head, and flanks of infected fish.

Aeromonas salmonicida is mostly associated with outbreak of "red-eye" ulcers in summer, when the water temperature rises above 72°F (22°C).

Erythrodermatitis of carp are bacteria transmitted by water; therefore, overcrowded ponds and handling infected fish will exacerbate the problem. Parasites like *Argulus* and flukes may also introduce the disease into a pond.

Bacterial hemorrhagic septicemia is caused by various motile *Aeromonas* species, such as *Aeromonas hydrophila*. Motile bacteria are part of normal water microflora, but under poor water conditions they can overcome the fish's defense system, with tragic consequences. The signs include ulcer-like lesions of the skin and muscle, necrosis (death of cells) in the fins and tail, exophthalmus (pop-eye), and dropsy. Antibiotic treatments are not very effective and it is best to remove the infected fish from the pond and dispose of it humanely.

Treatment for bacterial infections: Affected fish should be removed from the pond and treated in a quarantine tank. This will limit the possibility of further infections while allowing the patient to be given special care and treatment. The water quality in the quarantine tank must be maintained with daily partial water changes or adequate biological filtration. Maintain a salt concentration of 0.3–0.6 percent (see page 134).

An antibacterial agent, like potassium permanganate, can be used to clear the gills of necrotic tissue. Ulcers must be properly cleaned, making sure that all necrotic tissue is removed. Disinfect the wound and allow it to heal by checking and dressing it daily. If you are unsure of how to do this, seek expert advice from a veterinarian or koi specialist.

Avoid antibiotics unless the value of the fish justifies it, a sensitivity test is done, and the correct dosage and treatment regime is applied, as instructed by a fish expert.

Viral diseases

Koi are susceptible to many viruses, but those that cause high mortalities are of most concern to breeders and koi farms.

Spring viremia of carp (SVC) causes loss of young fish in spring when water temperatures rise from 50°F to 68°F (10°C–20°C). Above 68°F (20°C) mortalities usually cease. SVC is endemic to continental Europe but has found its way to many carp-producing countries and is classified as a notifiable disease by the World Organization for Animal Health (known as OIE).

Carp pox, a smooth, wax-like area on the skin, has the doubtful honor of being the oldest documented fish disease. It is activated when the water temperature falls below 57°F (14°C). Because of its disfiguring effect, carp pox may reduce the value of a particular koi. Even though it is not very infectious, fish with carp pox should not be bought, but it is not essential to remove fish carrying it from your collections.

Hikui, or red cancer, a disease of the red pigment cells on the epidermis, has a disfiguring effect on otherwise healthy fish. Areas in the red pattern become discolored and appear ulcerated or blistered, although the disfiguration does not seem to go deeper than the dermis. Sarcoma (cancer) of pigment cells in fish is not uncommon, but *hikui* is believed to have a viral origin, as antiviral treatments seem to contain the spread. Fish with *hikui* should not be used for breeding as they may pass the disease to their offspring.

Koi herpes virus (KHV) is a viral disease of great significance to the koi industry, as there is no cure for it. Since its first appearance in the 1990s, it has spread throughout the world. The disease is restricted to koi and carp, occurs at temperatures of 64°F–82°F (18–28°C), has an incubation period of 7–14 days, and a mortality rate above 80 percent.

An affected fish appears lethargic and swims with erratic movements until it finally just hangs motionless and dies. Some fish may have sunken eyes. Necrosis of the gill tissue, increased mucus secretion, and external and internal hemorrhaging are the most common clinical signs. The gills, kidneys, and hepatopancreas are carriers of viral particles.

KHV is transported in water and can stay active for about 24 hours without a host, allowing it to spread by seepage through groundwater. Fears that birds and animals can transmit the disease are probably overexaggerated.

To protect against KHV, all newly acquired fish should be quarantined for three weeks at a temperature of 73°F (23°C) (see page 134). If no symptoms are noticed during this time, the fish is probably not infected. To make doubly sure, an expert can perform a PCR test on a small gill snip, or take a swab, to confirm the absence of viral particles (see page 134). If KHV is detected, the affected fish should be disposed of humanely.

If any fish is dies unexpectedly, it can be dissected and pea-sized samples of the kidney, liver, and gills sent for testing to determine the cause of death.

This fish is suffering from carp pox; the lesions are clearly visible as white patches.

Quarantine

A treatment or quarantine tank is an essential item for serious koi-keepers. A typical tank has a capacity of 50-265 gallons (200-1,000 L) of water and should be equipped with a primed biological filter, heater, and adjustable thermostat. The quarantine tank must have its own set of handling nets and bowls that are not used in the main koi pond. It is also a good idea to be able to bypass the biological filter and have some means to do rapid partial water changes.

One way of quarantining fish is to maintain a 0.3-0.6 percent salt concentration in the tank (6½-13 pounds/3-6 kg coarse, noniodized salt per 265 gallons/1,000 L; 2.5-5 pounds per 100 gallons, or about 3 teaspoons per gallon).

All new fish should be quarantined for three weeks before they are put into the main pond. Introduce the fish to the quarantine tank at about the same temperature it comes from. Then raise the temperature, by no more than two degrees in 24 hours, to 70-73°F (21-23°C) and maintain it there for the full period of quarantining. Observe the fish daily, being especially on the lookout for parasites, and treat accordingly. If KHV symptoms are suspected, get the fish tested by an expert without delay.

PCR tests

PCR, or polymerase chain reaction, which is used to confirm the presence of both KHV and SVC (see page 133), is an analytical technique that is widely used in genetic fingerprinting. In the test, an identifiable part of the DNA of an organism or viral particle is amplified using the DNA's replication process. The PCR test is extremely sensitive, so very little material is needed for positive identification.

Samples should be fixed in 75 percent ethanol and stored in a freezer until they can be sent on to a laboratory that specializes in these tests. Lately, improved analytical techniques allow dry swabs of gill tissue to be used for viral detection.

Your local koi club will be able to advise on where PCR tests can be done.

Keep a separate net for use in the quarantine pond in order to avoid cross-contamination.

This external pond could be used to isolate new fish until it is safe to introduce them to the main pond.

Salt

Salt, or sodium chloride (NaCl), is the one chemical treatment koi-keepers cannot do without. Salt is good for controlling parasites, relieving stress, stimulating slime production, reducing osmotic stress when the skin has been damaged, and reducing the toxicity of contaminants like nitrite and ammonia.

Noniodized coarse salt for human consumption is perfect. Sea salt, rock salt, and Kosher salt are good alternatives. Salt for agricultural use, swimming pools, and water softeners can be used, provided they have no additives or anticaking agents.

For therapeutic effect, a salt concentration of 0.3 percent is typically used. For treating parasites like *Trichodina, Costia, Chilodinella,* and *Glossatella,* up to 0.6 per cent salt may be required due to the resistance some parasites may have towards it.

Salt can simply be added to the main pond, and the treatment can go on indefinitely, as a low level of salt will not harm either the fish or the pond filter, although too much could kill sensitive plants and algae.

A pond thermometer is vital for checking water temperature.

Dips

Dips are generally more effective in ridding the koi of external parasites and bacteria than long-term baths. Although dips do induce stress in the fish, the high concentration of the dip makes it less likely that any parasites will survive. Dip treatments usually also stimulate mucus production, which helps to expel organisms from the skin.

Dip new arrivals before introducing them to the pond or quarantine tank. Observe the fish at all times during the dipping process; if they weaken they must be removed immediately from the dip before they lose consciousness. Plan the treatment, making sure everything is ready. Having a second person on hand with a stopwatch, to call the instructions out loudly, is a great help, especially the first time.

It is a good idea to keep a record of all treatments, whether to an individual fish or to the pond as a whole. A written record becomes an easy reference for future treatments, and will also be useful if you have to call in professional help.

Salt A dip in a 5 percent salt solution (6 ounces/gallon or 50 g/L) for 70 seconds can be a quick and effective way to strip parasites from a koi. Three successive dips 12 to 24 hours apart are recommended.

Magnesium sulfate and salt A mixture of 3 percent magnesium sulfate (Epsom salts, $MgSO_4$) and 0.7 percent salt is very effective as a 10-minute dip that will also eradicate gill fluke. Dissolve 10½ ounces (300 g) of $MgSO_4$ and 2½ ounces (70 g) of NaCl per 2½ gallons (10 L) of water.

Potassium permanganate Dip for seven minutes in a 3.8 g per 10-gallon (1 g per 10 L) solution. Three consecutive dips over a period of five days will not only kill most flukes and parasites, but will strip necrotic tissue from bacterially and fungally infected gills and ulcers. It is best to use this only on large fish as smaller, sick fish may be helped "over the edge."

Note: The metric system is widely used by the scientific and medical community, because it is standardized, easy to use, and has a lower risk of errors. Anyone applying treatments at home is advised to adopt this system. However, the first step is to know the volume of your pond in liters (see page 94).

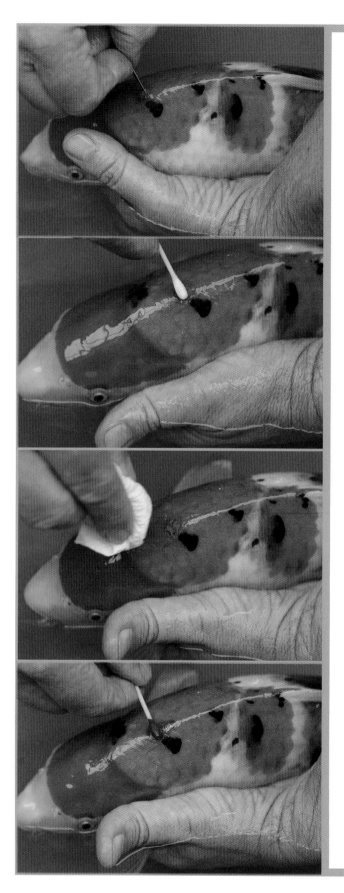

Treating an ulcer

Remove your watch and rings before handling koi. Get all the equipment ready and within reach; if it is your first time, it is a good idea to have a helper on standby. Anesthetize the fish only if it is difficult to handle.

Quickly remove all necrotic (dead) tissue from the wound and pull out any scales that might hide the infection. Using a scalpel or blade, scrape away all signs of infection or redness around the periphery of the wound, leaving it thoroughly clean. If this is done properly the first time, it won't have to be done again. If the infection is in bone or fin rays, cut them away or scrape clean; the tissue will regrow.

Disinfect the wound with an antiseptic and dab dry with paper towels. Apply a topical antiseptic, like tincture of iodine or mercurochrome, and dab dry. Seal the wound with a water-resistant ointment. Blow it dry and put the fish into the recovery basin, keeping watch until it has recovered and can be moved back to the quarantine tank. This should take less than a minute.

Maintain the quarantine tank with 0.3 percent salt solution at 68–75°F (20–24°C) to promote healing. Inspect the wound every day; if it was cleaned properly, it will soon heal. Any signs of hemorrhaging around the ulcer indicates the cleaning was inadequate, or the infection has advanced too far and the fish is having trouble maintaining internal water balance. In either case, contact a fish expert to administer an antibiotic and advise on further treatment.

How to anesthetize a fish

Prepare one 15-gallon (50 L) container with anesthetic and a second with clear, aerated water for recovery. Ensure the chemical is properly mixed before putting the fish into the tub. When the fish loses its sense of balance, it must be lifted out of the anesthetic and placed on a damp towel outside the tub. In the case of a small wound, one person can simply hold the fish while the other treats the wound or ulcer. If the fish shows signs of recovery during the treatment, put it back into the anesthetic again. Closely watch the fish's breathing, and do not restrict the operculum (gill openings, see illustration on page 23) while handling the fish.

Various anaesthetics have differing reaction times:

MS222: 50 mg/L (190 mg/gallon), ±3–5 minutes for it to take effect.

Quinaldine: 50 mg/L (190 mg/gallon), ±2–3 minutes for it to take effect.

2-phenoxyethynol: 25 ml/50 L (6⅕ tablespoons/gallon), ±2–4 minutes for it to take effect.

Clove oil: 5 drops/gallon (15 drops/10 L), ±10–12 minutes for it to take full effect, ±5–10 minutes to recovery.

Euthanasia/disposal

There are times when a decision has to be made to prevent further suffering by putting a fish out of its misery. The most humane way is to prepare some anesthetic and leave the fish in the solution until it stops breathing. If local ordinances allow it, the fish can then be buried in the garden (at least 12 inches/30 cm deep); otherwise place it in a garbage bag and take it to a municipal incinerator or ask your local koi club about other appropriate disposal methods.

To catch koi for treatment, use a net (top) to scoop up the fish, before transferring it gently to a plastic crate or floating basket (above) in which the koi can swim during inspection and treatment.

COMMON DISEASE TREATMENTS

DRUG	USE FOR	DOSAGE	DURATION	COMMENTS
Coarse salt, kitchen salt, noniodized salt	Stress relief, external protozoan parasites	2½ lb/100 gal. 3 kg/1,000 L	2–3 weeks	Some resistant parasites may require double the dosage.
Potassium permanganate	External parasites, including flukes, external lesions, bacterial and fungal infections	7.5-15 mg/gal. 2-4 mg/L	Maintain "pinkness" for 10 hours by adding 7.5 mg/gal. (2 mg/L) doses when water turns brown	Use higher dosage in systems with a high stocking level.
Formalin (37%) (use with caution)	Fungus, bacteria and external protozoan parasites	1½ tsp./100 gal. 20 ml/1,000 L	Three treatments every second day	
Malachite green (zinc-free oxalate) (use with caution)	External parasites, fungus	0.4 mg/gal. 0.1 mg/ L	Continuous	Can be used with salt, Carcinogenic, but very effective; wear rubber gloves when handling.
Dimilin (use with caution) (may be illegal in parts of the US and Canada)	*Lernaea, Argulus, Ergasilus*	3.5 mg/gal. 1 mg/ L	Continuous for three days	Systemic action inhibiting chitin production of parasite.
M+F	Ich *(Ichthyophirius)*, most protozoan parasites	Malachite green 0.4 mg/gal.; 0.1 mg/L Formalin ⅜ tsp./100 gal. 5ml/1,000 L	Repeat after two days	The only effective knock-out treatment for ich. Will not exterminate cysts.
Dipterex (may be illegal in some parts of the US and Canada)	*Lernaea, Argulus, Ergasilus,* flukes, tapeworms	Hard water 3.5 mg/gal.; 1 mg/ L Soft water 1.75 mg/gal.; 0.5 mg/L	Continuous	Do not use below 65°F (18°C) or above 82°F (28°C).
Praziquantel	Flukes, tapeworms	7.5 mg/gal. 2 mg/L	Repeat after two days	
Furanace Prefuran	Antimicrobial, fin rot, bacterial gill disease, *Columnaris, Aeromanas* and *Pseudomonas*	0.4-0.75 mg/gal. 0.1-0.2 mg/L	Continuous	Effective one-time treatment for wide spectrum of bacteria, parasites and fungi.

First aid kit

A basic first aid kit should contain the following items:

• Soft towel or baby's changing mat to work on;

• Cotton swabs, cotton wool, paper towels;

• Sharp scissors (small and large), forceps, tweezers;

• Scalpel and blades (a student's dissecting kit is ideal);

• Small plastic bowls; spatula or spoons for mixing;

• Liquid household antiseptic;

• Iodine-based topical antiseptic cream;

• Small measuring beaker (10 or 20 ml) and/or syringes

• Waterproof wound dressing;

• Methylated spirits (denatured alcohol) to sterilize equipment;

• Magnifying glass for examining wounds;

• Large bag of coarse, noniodized salt;

• Proprietary anesthetic containing quinaldine, MS222 (tricaine methane sulfonate), or 2-phenoxyethanol.

Optional items include:

• Measuring cylinder;

• Small medicine scale;

• Household bucket for mixing treatments; stick for stirring;

• Treatment chemicals: Potassium permanganate, malachite green, formalin (37 percent solution);

• Ethanol (75–90 percent) for fixing samples;

• Microscope, 50X–500X magnification.

Creating a koi collection

No two koi collections are the same, as each one is shaped by a combination of personal preference, individual aspiration, and available budget.

Building a collection takes time, but experience brings the realization that it is often better to have a small, carefully nurtured collection of higher grade koi than a pond stocked to the brim with fish that barely meet the minimum requirement of their varieties.

Koi collections are inevitably born in the enthusiasm that follows the building of a small garden water feature. The pond will be stocked with cheap, colorful koi from the nearest aquatic pet shop. There will be little consideration for quality, only for "nice" fish. As fast as the koi die through overstocking, an ill-suited pond environment, inadequate water management, poor health, or overfeeding, they will be replaced with new additions. It is only when the pond owner despairs at the continuous losses and seeks professional advice that he or she learns about the need for a suitable pond environment for koi and about "good" as opposed to "nice" fish.

Manabu Ogata of Ogata Koi Farm in Japan has identified six types of koi-keepers. At the bottom are beginners who keep fish as casual pets. One level up are those who have become intrigued and wish to learn more about koi and obtain better quality fish. Another rung up are koi-keepers who enter their fish in shows with the intention of comparing both their koi and their koi grooming skills against other fish and keepers.

Next comes the keeper who, usually just before a show, buys a superlative koi with the sole intention of winning a prize. The fifth category is the investor-keeper who acquires young fish with future potential, from which the best are kept and the rest sold off. Finally, in a class of their own, are keepers who acquire *tategoi* (young fish with good future potential), then foster their development so that show winners will eventually emerge. This last kind of koi-keeper takes pride in his or her collection as well as in koi-keeping skills.

Judging by the number of *tategoi* owned by koi-keepers, one might assume that, worldwide, breeders have mastered the skill of producing numerous young koi with the potential to become show champions. However, this is far from the truth. Dedicated breeders might set aside less than half a percent of a spawning as true *tategoi*, those rare, and highly valued, fish which generally achieve their pinnacle of excellence only in adult life.

Unscrupulous dealers, on the other hand, tend to label young koi as *tategoi* if they show any likelihood of improving in color, pattern, and size, even if not necessarily to the level of quality required to make them show winners.

Professional breeders are often reluctant to sell their *tategoi* to dealers, preferring to grow the fish on or make them available to keepers with sophisticated koi-keeping skills (as well as the financial means to purchase such treasured koi). For the most part, the so-called *tategoi* in a dealer's shop must be seen for what they are, a dealer's personal preference of young koi obtained from a breeder's agent or a wholesale exporter.

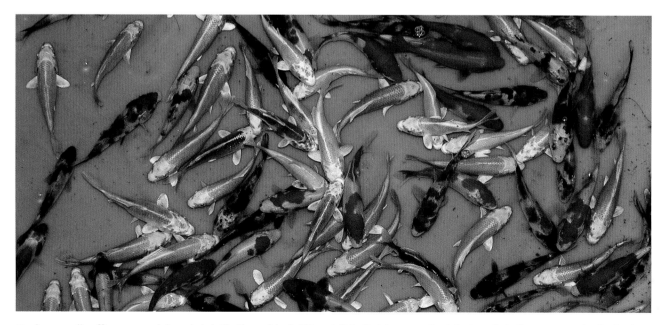

Dealers usually offer commercial-grade koi, like these 4 inch (10 cm) fish, that have survived the breeder's first two rounds of selection.

Starting a collection

The best advice for anyone who wants to create a decent koi collection with long-term value is to build up a nucleus of fish that will develop over time, while incorporating some specimens with immediate appeal. The sensible collector will invest in young koi with the potential to achieve and maintain their quality in the future. Less savvy collectors will buy koi that have already achieved a state of finish that can rarely be improved upon and is likely to deteriorate in quality.

A collection from which koi-keepers can gain both pleasure and reward will feature mainly small to medium-sized koi that meet most of the requirements of their varieties, a few that would do their varieties justice at a show and perhaps one or two—often a *Chagoi, Soragoi*, or *Ogon*—that will grow big and become the "king of the pond" because of its imposing presence. What most collections lack, usually because of their high cost, is a *tategoi* with the potential to develop very slowly into a show winner when it is five years old or older.

Buying from a dealer

Dealers usually separate their koi into ponds according to grade and price. The grading systems differ from supplier to supplier and country to country, but usually can be separated into commercial (lowest commercial grade), select (highest commercial grade), show grade (usually indicating show quality), and young koi considered *tategoi*. The commercial grades are often subdivided into two or three lower grades of fish that perhaps should not have been put onto the market.

Prices vary according to size, quality, and availability. If a koi has been imported, the cost will include freight expenses and customs duties, as well as the dealer's markup.

Fashion also influences price and this particularly applies to the variety that the ZNA (see page 153) selects to promote annually. The heightened attention to that variety, and the quest for perfect specimens, can unfairly inflate prices.

Some fish have an inflated commercial value purely because of global demand. For example, a koi with any sort of round *tancho* (see page 67) marking on the head will fetch a high

price irrespective of its innate qualities. All koi-keepers want such a fish in their pond and the dealers know it. Fish with attributed bloodlines, or those bought from the agent of a famous-name breeder, may also carry a higher price. However, koi are generally not sold with a certified pedigree, and buyers should be wary of the validity of bloodline claims. Koi purporting to come from a famous breeder might not necessarily have been bred by him, because many breeders buy in fish from small koi farmers to supplement their own stock.

Experienced koi-keepers prefer to select a few dealers with whom to build a relationship of trust, based on the dealer's knowledge of his koi's origins, as well as their present and future quality; information that any scrupulous dealer will happily, generously, and honestly share. Provided a dealer has been honest with his or her assumptions, there can be no recriminations later. However, once a purchase is made, it is up to the koi-keeper to provide the optimum pond environment and level of care that will allow the koi to develop to its full potential. It is the easiest thing in the world to destroy the qualities of a good koi through poor pond management.

Dealers separate different size fish into individual ponds for convenience and ease of handling.

Guidelines for selecting koi

One of the most basic guidelines for selecting koi with qualities that will remain stable or even improve as they grow is to know the carrying capacity of your pond (see page 95). This figure must take into account the present body mass of the total number of fish in your collection as well as being able to accommodate increases in body mass as they grow.

In an overstocked pond, the fish simply will not grow as fast or as big as they would have in a pond with adequate space. The ideal is to place similarly sized fish in the same pond in order to equalize the competition for food and promote uniform growth, but this is rarely possible.

If you intend to show your koi, then, when purchasing new fish, eliminate from contention any with obvious faults and flaws. Faults include deformities, nondesirable colors, or unwanted markings, and are always discriminated against at a show. Flaws, usually of scalation, markings, and patterns, might appear insignificant and tolerable on smaller fish but they tend to become more pronounced as the fish grows.

Finishing koi for sale

Although young koi are affordable, they may disappoint serious collectors. Small koi sold by dealers are usually brightly colored, with striking patterns, but neither feature is likely to survive as the fish ages.

Small fish are often deliberately finished for the market. When they were hauled out of their mud dams, they would have shown subdued colors and messy patterns. Because mud dam space is precious, only the best koi are grown on there, so commercial-grade koi tend to be sold off quickly to create better conditions for the top-grade fish.

Young, commercial-grade koi are moved into deep concrete ponds with cold water that is heavily aerated. They are fed color-enhancing food to make them color up very quickly. They do not grow much, but their body shape and color mature faster than would be the case in a mud dam. Fish that are not sold may spend a second season in these cramped conditions, making them two-year-old miniature specimens with brilliant colors and mature bodies—of high commercial value but with no prospects for further growth.

The ideal is to keep similarly sized fish in the same pond, to minimize the competition for food.

Early finishing inevitably means that growth is sacrificed. A beautifully finished 6-8 inches (15-20 cm) young koi in a dealer's pond will probably be 12-18 months old. With an unbroken stay in a mud dam, it might have been able to reach 8-12 inches (20-30 cm) and probably would have developed a better body shape.

Selection criteria

While there is nothing wrong with having a collection of small, beautiful koi, it is wrong to expect them to retain their appeal for years to come. It makes more sense to select fish with some immediate appeal plus the promise of more to come later. Things to watch out for include:

Sumi **pattern** Focus on young fish with a big pattern. Koi do not gain pattern with age, so a pattern that is too small in a youngster will become progressively fragmented relative to the rest of the body as the fish grows. The pattern need not be complete and defined in a young fish, especially if *sumi* is one of the colors, as *sumi* takes time to emerge and stabilize.

The *sumi* in *Sanke* could either be *kasane-zumi* (where it overlaps the *hi* and does not touch the white ground at all), or *tsubo-zumi* (where the *sumi* just touches the *hi* markings or is standing alone on the white skin). Well-defined *kasane-zumi* can punctuate a pattern and be very appealing. *Tsubo-zumi* helps to give cohesion to the pattern, bridging *hi* markings and "filling in" the white ground. It is easier to finish *tsubo-sumi* than *kasane-zumi*.

A *Sanke* with a bold *sumi* marking between the *hi* marking on the head and the first body marking is said to have *kata-sumi* and creates an impression of strength. A young *Sanke* with *kata-zumi* should be favored.

Selecting young *Showa* and *Utsurimono* is difficult, because their *sumi* only develops later in life. In these youngsters, the *sumi* will be obscured and unattractive. Avoid *sumi* with an overall gray appearance. Favor the blue-black type of *sumi*; even if most of it lies submerged, some parts of the pattern should already show up solid and defined.

In young *Showa*, the *hi* and white should dominate the *sumi*, which is usually bluish gray at first, only emerging and maturing later. The best indicator of the quality of *sumi* in both *Showa* and *Utsurimono* is the definite, bold presence of *sumi* in the pectoral fins. Known as *motoguro*, this might cover a large area of the fin but will usually tidy up with age.

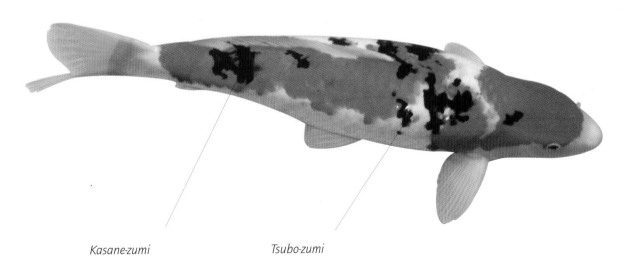

Kasane-zumi   Tsubo-zumi

Sumi *takes time to emerge and stabilize, so select young fish whose* sumi *will improve as they age.*

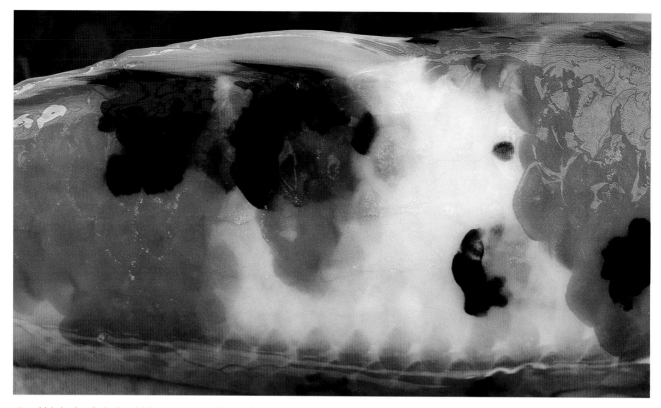

Good hi *(red color) should be even and thick, with clearly discernable outlines; good* sumi *(black color) should be solid and well-defined. The white ground should be thick and clear, without a gray or amber tinge. The* kiwa *should be sharp and the* sashi *deep.*

Good *hi* A one- to two-year-old koi already revealing sharply defined bright red markings is sure to lose its appeal quickly. As the *hi* has been achieved by early finishing, it will probably be unstable. Orange-colored *hi* indicates better quality in later development. This applies to young *Kohaku, Sanke, Showa, Goromo*, and, to some extent, *Goshiki*.

Of the two kinds of *hi* (see page 36) the purple-based has depth and density but lacks refinement. Although orange-based *hi* is more difficult to mature and finish, once achieved, it has a refinement the other cannot emulate.

Provided both the koi and the pond both receive optimum attention, orange-based *hi* will develop well over a period of years, deepening as if color is being added layer by layer, while gaining luster at the same time. This is especially true of female fish that tend to finish much later in their adult life.

Irrespective of the hue, the *hi* should be even and thick. The individual scales within the markings should not be easily distinguishable and there should be a sharp edge (*kiwa*) on the posterior side of the marking.

White ground If a koi has a white ground, it must be snow white, with preference given to fish with thick white on the face and head. Far too many *Kohaku, Sanke, Shiro Bekko*, and *Shiro-Utsuri* display white that is gray- or amber-tinted.

Some koi-keepers ignore poor white ground in favor of excellent quality of the *hi* and *sumi*. Regardless of how good the *hi* or *sumi* is, it is their quality, in tandem with the quality of the white, that determines excellence. A koi with a poor white ground can never have long-lasting, quality *hi*.

Disease and deformity

When selecting koi of any size, before considering esthetic features like color or pattern, eliminate those koi that show any symptom of disease. Not only is there the risk of introducing disease into your pond, but a fish that is not healthy will never be an asset to your collection. Sick fish swim in a lethargic or whip-like manner, or might lie at the bottom of the pond. The body may be thin or the head appear out of proportion. The gills could be swollen, or the fins frayed.

If you want to show your fish, do not consider buying a koi with poor body shape. Viewed from the side or above, the ideal body is torpedo-shaped, or tapered toward the head and tail, and oval, rather than round, in circumference.

Eliminate from contention any fish with visible deformities, such as missing barbels or crooked heads and mouths. Head deformities are especially prevalent amongst *Showa* and *Shiro-Utsuri*, where the black coloring can obscure features.

Do not mistake pot bellies for gravid (pregnant) female koi. A fat-bellied fish will not score any points in a show. Reject koi showing scars where scales are absent; although missing scales can regenerate, the new ones might be of different hue and shape.

Gender and shape

Female koi are more prized than males. They have a better body shape and exceed males in size, although males grow faster in their first few years and achieve a quicker finish. Females are slow to mature, but retain their qualities for longer. Generally, only experienced koi-keepers can determine gender in fish under two years of age.

If young fish cannot be sexed in order to identify the females, then indicators of potential size must be sought. The first of these is a thick peduncle (the area between the end of the dorsal fin and the start of the tail fin). Another guideline is the height and shape between the abdomen and the shoulder ridge. The higher this is, the greater the koi's potential to grow big. The back should have a slightly rounder arch than the abdominal line. However, if the highest point of the shoulder is the anterior root rather than the middle portion of the base of the dorsal fin, the body will be dome-shaped, with too long a slope toward the tail.

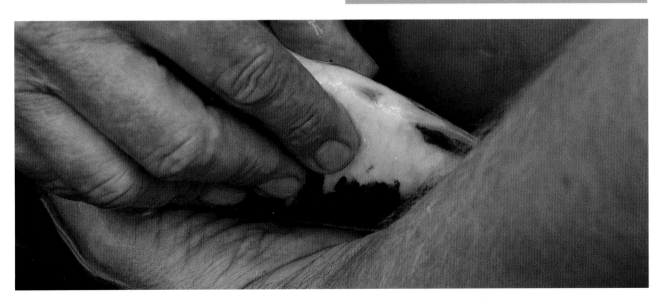

To check gender, a breeder milks a fish to determine whether milt is present, in which case the fish is male.

Selecting the right size koi

What size koi are best for your pond? For convenience, most koi-keepers identify five sizes: mini, small, medium, large, and jumbo. Pond size is an important element in determining the number of koi you should keep (see page 95). Overstocking makes the fish susceptible to disease as well as inhibiting their natural development and growth.

Mini koi Fish under 8 inches (20 cm) in length are ideal for ponds up to 265 gallons (1,000 L) capacity, provided there is adequate filtration and aeration. They may already have colored up and have good patterns, or could be in the process of development. Their growth rate is fast and the continuous changes in color and pattern can be a constant source of fun. The majority of mini koi will not come to much as they grow into the next size group, and their colors and patterns can erode or even fade away completely.

Small koi These are 8–14 inches (20–35 cm) in length and make up the majority of hobbyist koi collections. Their color and patterns will have stabilized and the fish gained some resistance to disease, which makes them easier to keep. Small koi can have further growth potential.

Medium koi More experienced keepers favor fish 14–16 inches (35–40 cm) long as the pattern has stabilized. Their finish can be promoted by feeding color-enhancing food in con-trolled quantities. Take particular care to avoid injuries or scarring which, at this age and size, take a long time to heal. The minimum pond volume for a small collection of medium-size koi is 2,640 gallons (10,000 L).

Large koi The prices of fish in the 25–30 inch (65–75 cm) size group mean that few koi-keepers can afford them. These impressive fish have powerful bodies, pattern, and color and their swimming movement is majestic, but they require a pond with a minimum volume of 7,925 gallons (30,000 L).

Jumbo koi Reaching 28 inches (70 cm) and over, these must be housed in a pond with a depth of at least 6.5 feet (2 m) and a volume in excess of 13,200 gallons (50,000 L)—something the average koi-keeper is seldom able to accomplish.

Serious koi-keepers are never satisfied that their collection is complete, and enthusiasts are usually on a perpetual quest to acquire better fish. Space for new additions is created through natural deaths, losses brought on by human error, and selling or giving away koi that fall short of expectations.

For serious collectors, pond space is too valuable to be claimed by inferior-quality koi. Fish that have lost color, pattern, or body shape, or have prominent scars, should be removed from a collection. New homes can usually be found among novice koi-keepers who would welcome a few free fish.

Large koi require a big, deep pond and carefully controlled numbers to bring out their majesty and grace.

Should I breed my koi?

At some stage, almost every koi-keeper will be tempted to spawn their fish. But before doing so, they should consider the wisdom and ethics of random breeding without a specific purpose. Professional koi breeders routinely cull undesirable fry, but koi-keepers might want to keep all the fry alive, even those with faults. This will simply strain the pond's resources and make it hard to raise a crop of healthy mature fish.

Furthermore, spawning is a robust process and inexperienced koi-keepers might not be able to limit injuries or even prevent the death of one or more parent fish. If you really want to breed your koi, seek expert advice and start slowly.

When it comes to lineage, hobbyist koi-keepers should never dabble with the genetics of koi by trying to breed a "new" variety to satisfy their own preferences. Breeding new varieties takes years of careful cross-matching and should only be done by specialists in koi bloodlines and genetics.

Tips for breeders

Koi-keepers who are committed to breeding should take the following to heart:

• Select koi parents with the best attributes of their variety. Pretty koi parents do not necessarily make pretty babies, so choose parent fish on the strength of their body shapes, good-quality color, and good scalation rather than looks alone.

• Do not use show-quality koi for breeding; they will suffer bruises, cuts, torn fins, and missing scales, as well as stress during spawning.

• Get both parent fish into prime health before spawning and again afterward.

• Cull the fry. Few varieties breed true, and every poor specimen must be weeded out in order to strengthen, not weaken, the gene pool.

• Don't make errors. An entire breeding can be wiped out through carelessness and oversight.

• Keep notes and records for future attempts. Above all, do not expect a breeding to produce multiple champions. One breeder, using bloodline parent stock, calculated that after three cullings he would retain about 600 youngsters out of every 100,000 fry, of which only 20 would be potential show koi.

Choose potential breeding stock for its conformation to the best attributes of the specific variety, not just on looks alone. That way, the best genes will be passed on.

Glossary

absorption The taking in of one substance by another, including, in animals, various gases, fluids, etc., through the mucus membranes or the skin (much as a sponge retains water).

adsorption The adherence of one substance, usually a gas, to the solid surface of another substance.

aerobic Depending on free oxygen.

ago-hi The *hi* markings on the cheeks of *Asagi* and *Shusui*.

ai Blue (indigo) color.

Aigoromo Koi with blue-robed scales on a *hi* pattern.

Ai-Showa Alternative name for *Koromo-Showa*.

aka Red (when referring to ground).

Aka-Bekko *Bekko* with a red ground.

Akabo *Kohaku* with red all over.

Aka-Hajiro *Kohaku* with a red body and white tips to the pectoral fins.

Aka-Matsuba Koi with *matsuba* scalation on a red ground.

Akamuji Koi with red or orange covering the entire body and fins, not favored, removed during culling.

Aka-Sanke *Sanke* with a red body and *sumi* markings but a white nose and abdomen.

albino Any animal lacking pigment. Albino koi characteristically have pink eyes; a white koi with black eyes is not albino.

alkalinity The total of substances in water, mainly carbonate and hydroxyl ions, which maintain the pH level above 7.0.

anaerobic Not dependent on free oxygen to function.

anoxic A lack or absence of oxygen.

ara-doitsu *Doitsu* koi with only a scattering of *doitsu* scales.

Asagi Koi with a light and dark blue ground with red markings on the jaw and abdomen.

Asagi-Magoi Blue-black carp.

Asagi-Sanke *Asagi* with a pale blue back, red head, and red flanks and a pure white lower abdomen.

Asagi-Suminagashi Alternative name for *Suminagashi*.

bara-zumi Small, scattered *sumi* markings. Also see *jari-zumi*.

Bekko Koi with a "stepping stone" pattern of black markings on a white, red, or yellow ground.

beni Dark red.

Benigoi Koi with a vermillion red ground all over.

Beni-Kujaku *Kujaku* in which the *hi* covers all of the body.

beta-gin *Ginrin* scalation in which the entire scale glitters.

biomass Microorganisms that break down waste and remove toxins; vegetable matter used as a source of energy.

boke When the *sumi* scales appear blurred.

bongiri *Kohaku* with a strong *hi* pattern on the front part of the body, extending to the head.

Bongoi Koi of average quality. Also called *chuppa*.

boze *Kohaku* with no *hi* marking on the head.

bu The size grouping at a koi show.

budo Grape-like purplish clusters of scales.

Budo-Goromo Koi with wine-colored scales arranged as clusters of grapes on a *hi* pattern.

Budo-Sanke Alternative name for *Budo-Goromo*.

cha Color brown as in "tea."

Chagoi Koi with a brown (turmeric yellow) ground all over.

chara-gin *Dia-gin* with tinsel gold appearance.

chigyo Small fry.

chitai The ground (base color) of a koi.

choman Tumor of the reproductive organs.

dagoi Koi of poor quality. Also called *dari*.

daiya Diamond-like *ginrin* also known as Hiroshima-*Ginrin*.

danmoyo Stepped pattern.

dia-gin *Ginrin* scalation with diamond-like reflecting characteristics. Also called Diamond-*Ginrin*.

dohmaki Pattern extending below the lateral line.

doitsu Scaleless koi. Also see *kagami-goi* and *kawa-goi*.

doro-zumi Mud-black color.

ecosystem The natural interactions and systems in a pond that keep the surrounding environment in balance.

ectoparasites Parasites that live on the body of a fish.

edome To stop feeding.

endoparasites Parasites that live inside the fish.

epithelium The layer of cells that form on the outer surface of the skin and gills.

ezuke To give food.

Fuji-Kohaku *Kohaku* with silver white lumps (*fuji*) on the head.

fukurin The skin between the scales which gives it a shiny edge and net effect.

genotype The genetic makeup of an individual or population sharing a specific constitution.

gin Metallic white, which appears as silver.

Gin-Bekko Koi with the *Bekko* pattern on a platinum ground.

Ginbo Koi of *Ogon* variety with a silver metallic sheen on dark ground, considered low quality. Also known as a Ghost.

Gin-Matsuba *Matsuba* scalation on a platinum ground.

ginrin Iridescent scalation.

Gin-Shiro *Shiro-Utsuri* with a platinum sheen.

Gin-Showa *Showa* with a platinum or metallic silver sheen.

Ginsui *Shusui* with a silver sheen.

go Five.

-goi Koi or carp, as part of a word, not used in isolation.

goma Small black spot.

gosanke "The top three." The grouping of *Kohaku*, *Sanke*, and *Showa*.

Goshiki A five-colored koi.

Goshiki-han Small *hi* markings in the pectoral fins of *Goshiki*.

Goshiki-Shusui *Goshiki* with the *doitsu* (scaleless) dark blue ground typical of *Shusui*.

gotenzakura Pattern of small clusters of red scales resembling cherry blossoms in bloom.

ground The base color of a koi's body.

hachi Head or head marking.

Hachibi Early name for a *menkaburi Kohaku*.

hachi-zumi Lightning-shaped *sumi* marking on the head.

hachiware *Sumi* head marking on *Showa*, extending from the nose to the shoulder.

hadaji Skin of Koi.

Hage-Shiro Koi with a black body with white tips to the pectoral fins and white on the nose that spreads over the head.

Hajiro "White wings." Koi with a black body, with white on the tips of the pectoral fins only.

Hana-Shusui *Shusui* in which a second line of *hi* runs between the lateral line and the dorsal line.

hana-zumi A *sumi* marking on the nose and mouth area.

hanatsuki A *hi* marking on the head extending to the mouth.

hara-aka Red color on the abdomen.

hara-hi Red color on the abdomen. Also the *hi* markings on the abdomen and flanks of *Asagi* and *Shusui*.

Hariwake Koi with a pattern combining gold and platinum except those out of the *Utsurimono* lineage.

Heisei Nishiki Preferred name for *doitsu Yamatonishiki* (in honor of the Heisei era).

hi Red (as a color, marking, or pattern).

Hi Kage-Utsuri *Hi-Utsuri* with the white ground revealing *kage* scalation.

Hi-Asagi *Asagi* with *hi* covering all of the back.

Higoi Koi with a red-orange ground color.

Hikari-Moyomono All metallic koi with patterns of two or more colors other than those bred out of the *Utsuri*-types.

Hikari-Mujimono Koi with single metallic colors and their *matsuba* variations.

Hikari-Utsurimono The metallic versions of *Showa* and *Utsurimono*.

Hi-Ogon Koi with a red-gold ground color.

Hi-Showa *Showa* with a dominant *hi* marking stretching from nose to tail, with little intrusions of white.

Hi-Shusui *Shusui* in which the red of the abdomen extends upward to cover all of the back.

Hi-Utsuri *Utsuri* with a red ground.

hoaka A *hi* marking on the gill plate.

hon-zumi The *sumi* of *Sanke*.

honzome *Kiwa* where the *hi* stands out in bold relief on the edges of the scale.

hoo-kazuki Early red mutation among carp.

hoshi Window within a pattern or small, isolated patches of *sumi*.

ikeage "The Harvest." The tradition of harvesting the ponds.

inazuma Lightning bolt or zigzag pattern.

ippon-hi Continuous, unvaried marking reaching from the head to the base of the tail.

iridocytes Color cells with reflective properties.

iro na shiagari The best condition, texture, and sheen of color.

jari-zumi Small, scattered *sumi* markings.

jiro White.

kado Edge.

kado-gin *Ginrin* scalation in which only the posterior edge of the scale glitters.

kagami-goi Mirror (*doitsu*) carp with no scales at all.

kage Hazy or "phantom" pattern of the ground color.

Kage-Showa *Showa* with white ground over *kage* scalation.

kanoko Fawn-like, dappled *hi* scales on white ground.

Kanoko-Kohaku Dappled *hi* scalation on a *Kohaku*.

Kanoko-Sanke Dappled *hi* scalation on a *Sanke*.

Kanoko-Showa Dappled *hi* scalation on a *Showa*.

karasu Black, as in "crow."

Karasugoi Koi that is black all over.

kasane-zumi *Sumi* markings overlapping onto *hi* markings.

kasu-gin *Ginrin* scalation that has an irregular arrangement of glitter along the edge of the scale.

kata-moyo Patterning on only one side of the body.

kata-zumi Big, bold black marking on a shoulder.

katsubera "Shoehorn." Odd-shaped head markings.

kawa-goi Leather (*doitsu*) carp with large reflective scales.

Kawarimono A grouping of varieties of nonmetallic koi.

ki Yellow.

Ki-Bekko *Bekko* with a yellow ground.

Kigoi Koi with a yellow ground color.

Kikusui A *doitsu Kohaku* crossed with a Platinum-*Ogon*. Like a *doitsu Hariwake* but with red pattern.

Ki-Matsuba Koi with *matsuba* scalation on a yellow ground.

kin Metallic yellow, which appears as gold.

Kin Ki-Utsuri *Ki-Utsuri* with a golden sheen.

Kinbo Koi of *Ogon* variety with a slight golden metallic sheen on dark ground, considered low quality.

kindai Modern.

Kindai-Goshiki *Goshiki* with a more pronounced *Asagi* patterning of dark blue robing.

Kindai Showa *Showa* showing substantially more white ground, smaller/fewer *sumi*, and smaller *hi*.

Kinginrin Koi of all the varieties, which display shiny scales across the length of the back.

Kin-Matsuba *Matsuba* scalation on a ground color of gold.

Kin-Showa *Showa* with a golden sheen.

Kinsui Gold-sheen *Shusui*.

kinzakura Metallic version of *gotenzakura*.

Ki-Shusui A yellow *Shusui* with blue on the back.

Ki-Utsuri *Utsuri* with a yellow ground.

kiwa Border between the posterior edge of a marking and the white ground.

Kohaku Koi with red markings on a white ground.

Koi-dangi Koi keepers enthusiastically talking about koi.

Koishi The breeders of Koi.

kokenami Rows of precisely aligned, regular scales.

kokesuki A scale that is paler in color or has lost all color.

Kokugyo "National Fish." Koi.

komoyo Smaller-size markings.

Konjo-Asagi *Asagi* with intense indigo-colored scales.

Koromo Koi with scales robed in blue or black, on red markings, that create a mesh-like pattern.

Koromo-Sanke Hybrid of the *Aigoromo* and *Sanke*.

Koromo-Sanshoku Alternative name for *Goromo-Sanke*.

Koromo-Showa Hybrid of the *Aigoromo* and *Showa*.
koromo-zumi The *sumi* of *koromo*.
kuchibeni Small lipstick-like mark on the upper lip.
Kujaku *Goshiki* with *Asagi* patterning on a platinum ground.
Kumonryu The *doitsu* version of *Karasugoi*.
kura Saddle-like marking across the back.
Kuro-Goshiki *Goshiki* with a ground of darker blue hue.
Kuro-Ki-Han Early ancestor koi with black ground color and white markings.
Kuroko The process by which black fry is selected when breeding *Showa* and *Utsuri*.
kuromakka *Hi* of a deep, blackish hue.

lateral line Sensory organs on each side of a koi's body. The main function is to detect vibrations in the water.

mado-aki White ground breaking through into the *hi* marking as a distinctive window.
Magoi Wild brown-black and blue-black carp, also cultivated for food, the original ancestor of koi.
maki-agari Pattern extending from the abdomen upward.
maki-komi Pattern extending from the back downward.
Mameshibori-Goshiki Alternative name for *Kindai-Goshiki*.
maruten A *hi* marking on the head, more or less round and separated from the rest of the *hi* pattern.
maruzome *Kiwa* where the *hi* stands out in bold relief on the edges of the scale.
matsuba Scales appearing in relief and arranged in a pattern that resemble the seed-scales of a pine cone.
Matsuba-Doitsu Koi with the *doitsu* version of *matsuba* scalation.
Matsubagoi Koi with *matsuba* scalation.
Matsuba-Hariwake *Matsuba* scalation *Hariwake*.
Matsukawabake Koi of which the white and black pattern changes according to the seasons.
mekazura A *hi* marking on the head that covers the eyes or chin.
menkaburi Hooded. Where the red head marking covers all or most of the head.
menware Y-shaped *sumi* marking dividing the face in two.
mesu Female koi.
Midorigoi A green-colored hybrid koi.
miseba Focal point.
mitsu-kura Pattern of three saddle-like markings across the back.
mizu Water.
Mizu-Asagi *Asagi* of white-blue color. (Also known as *Akebi-Asagi* or *Water-Asagi*.)
mono A "thing" or "things."
motoaka Red color markings at the base of the fins.
motoguro Bold *sumi* marking on the pectoral fin, extending from the base and covering from a third to a half of the surface. Characteristic of *Showa* and *Utsurimono*.
moto-hi A *hi* mark extending to the base of the pectoral fin.
moyo Patterned.
muda-goke Single or clusters of superfluous *doitsu* scales.
muji Plain or single-colored.

nabe-zumi Charred-pan black color. Has a tendency to fade under stress conditions.
Narumi-Asagi *Asagi* in which the dark blue center of the scale has a pale blue surround.
nen'eki Mucus which covers the Koi.
Nezugoi Koi with a gray ground all over, *nezu* for "mouse."
nezumi Gray.
Nezu-Ogon Koi with a mouse-gray silver ground color. Also called *Nezumi-Ogon*.
ni Two.
niban-hi Secondary development of *hi*.
nidan Two-step pattern.
nidan-hi Two-stepped red markings.
Nishikigoi Alternative name for koi.
nitrification The oxidation of ammonia in pond water into nitrites and nitrates by bacterial action.
nitrifying bacteria Bacteria that break down fish waste from ammonia nitrite to nitrate.
nitrogen cycle A natural cycle relating to the transformation of nitrogen and nitrogenous compounds ensuring the availability of nitrogen to all forms of life.
nitrosomonas bacteria Oxygen-loving bacteria that oxidize total ammonia into nitrite.

Ochibashigure Koi with a pattern of dark brown markings on a ground color that varies from light gray to green to brown.
ochiru To die, to degenerate.
odome Area between the last red marking and the start of the tail.
ogon Saffron metallic sheen.
Ogon Koi with a gold metallic sheen.
Ogon-Utsuri *Aki-Utsuri* or *Hi-Utsuri* with a golden sheen. Also called *Kin-Shiro*.
oiboshi Small whitish lumps appearing on the gill plates of male koi during the breeding season.
ojima Black stripes on the tail fin, as in *Sanke*, *Bekko*, and *Utsurimono*.
ojime Refers to the last *hi* marking before the tail. Used in conjunction with *odome*.
omoyo Bigger size markings.
operculum The flap covering a koi's gills.
orenji Orange.
Orenji-Hariwake Koi with a platinum-colored pattern on a ground of orange-gold.
Orenji-Ogon *Ogon* with an orange-gold sheen.
osmoregulation A complex process by which fish maintain a constant level of salts within their body fluids.
osmosis The passage of a substance through a membrane from a weaker or less concentrated solution to a stronger one.
osu Male koi.
ozuke Peduncle, the scaled area just before the tail.

pathogen Any organism or substance that causes disease.
Pearl-Shusui *Shusui* with *fukurin* on the scales of the back.
peduncle The area between the dorsal and tail fins.
pH The recognized measurement of acidity and alkalinity. Pure water (neutral pH) is 7.0; acid solutions have a pH of less

than 7; alkaline solutions a pH greater than 7. (pH stands for "potential of hydrogen.")

phenotype The physical constitution of an organism as determined by the interaction of its genetic constitution and the environment. (Compare genotype).

platinum Silver ground color.

Platinum-Kohaku The "metallic" *Kohaku*. Also called *Kin-Fuji*.

Platinum-Ogon *Ogon* with a silver sheen. Also known as *Purachina*.

poikilothermic Having an internal (body) temperature that varies with, or is dependent upon, the temperature of the surroundings. Cold-blooded.

Purachina See *Platinum-Ogon*.

Ryogoi Koi of good quality.

saiko Gill rakers in the mouth used for filtering food particles.

Sakura-Ogon *Kanoko-Kohaku* with a metallic sheen.

sandan A three-step pattern.

Sanke Koi with red and black markings on a white ground.

Sanke-Shusui *Sanke* with the *doitsu* of *Shusui*.

Sarasa Carp with a white body and red on its back.

sashi Border between the anterior edge of a marking and the white ground.

sesame Very small *sumi* markings.

shima Black stripes on the pectoral fin.

shimmie Disfiguring black freckle.

Shinkokai All-Japan Nishikigoi Association for koi dealers and breeders.

shiri ga karui Too few markings on the rear.

shiri ga omoi Too heavy markings on the rear.

shiro White.

Shiro Kage-Utsuri *Shiro-Utsuri* with the white ground revealing *kage* scalation.

Shiro-Bekko *Bekko* with a white ground.

Shiro-Bo *Kohaku* with no trace of *hi*.

Shiro-Fuji All-white (*Shiro-Muji*) koi with luster on the head.

shiroji White base color.

Shiro-Matsuba Koi with *matsuba* scalation on white ground.

Shiromuji Koi with no color.

Shiromuji-dia All-white, nonmetallic koi with random *ginrin* scales.

Shiro-Ogon Koi with a whitish-gray silver ground color.

Shiro-Utsuri *Utsuri* with a white ground.

Shiryu Purple-colored koi.

Shizumi-zumi Submerged *sumi*. Also called *ato-zumi*.

Shochikubai *Aigoromo* with metallic sheen.

Showa Koi with heavy black markings on the head and body to complement the red markings, all on a white ground.

Showa-Sankshoku Original name for *Showa*. Literally "the three-colored koi that appeared in the Showa era."

Showa-Shusui *Showa* with the *doitsu* of *Shusui*.

Shusui *Doitsu* version of the *Asagi*.

Shusui-bire The *hi* markings on the pectoral fins of *Asagi* and *Shusui*.

Soragoi Koi with a blue-gray ground all over. *Sora* means "blue like the sky."

Sudare-gin *Ginrin* scalation where the glitter radiates out from the edge to the inner part.

sumi Black color.

Sumi-Goromo Koi with black-robed scales on a *hi* pattern.

Suminagashi *Karasugoi* with an *Asagi* pattern on the black.

SVC Spring viremia of carp; a viral disease that occurs in spring, when the water temperature remains below 60°F (15°C).

Taisho-Sanshoku Original name for *Sanke*. Literally "the three-colored koi that appeared in the Taisho era."

Taki-Asagi *Asagi* with a white break separating the *hi* on the abdomen from the blue back.

Tama-gin *Ginrin* scalation that has glittering round centers. (Also known as *Pearl-Ginrin* and *Tsubo-gin*.)

tancho Red circular marking on the head only.

Tancho Koi of all the varieties and subvarieties, which display a single circular red marking on the head.

tategoi Young fish with the potential to achieve excellence as it matures.

teaka Red spots on the tail of a *Kohaku*.

tejima Black lines (stripes) extending from the base of the pectoral fin but not quite reaching the tips.

Tetsu-Magoi Brown-black carp.

tobi-hi Small *hi* marking isolated from the main pattern.

Tora-Ogon *Ki-Bekko* on a gold ground.

tosai Yearling koi.

tsubo-zumi *Sumi* markings on the white ground.

tsukidashi A *hi* marking on the head extending onto the mouth.

urushi-zumi Best quality *sumi*, lacquer-like in appearance.

Utsurimono The grouping of koi with a white, red, or yellow ground onto which a bold, often continuous, *sumi* pattern is laid.

wagoi Normal, full-scaled.

water quality A measure of the suitability of water for a particular use, i.e., for keeping koi.

yamabuki Yellow-gold.

Yamabuki-Hariwake Koi with a platinum-colored pattern on a ground of lemon-gold.

Yamabuki-Ogon *Ogon* with a yellow-gold sheen.

Yamatonishiki *Sanke* with a metallic sheen.

yogyo Young koi.

yondan Four-step pattern.

Yotsujiro Koi with a black body with a white head and white on the tail and pectoral fins.

Yugoi Koi of excellent quality. Also called *pongoi*.

Zen Nippon Airinkai The Japan-based international promoter of koi-keeping. Abbreviated to ZNA.

zobonuhaki Red pattern that almost covers the rear half as though the koi is wearing red pants.

Index

References

Boyd, C.E. *Water Quality in Ponds for Aquaculture*, Birmingham Publishing Co., 1990.

Boyd, C.E. *Water Quality Management for Pond Fish Culture*, Elsevier Scientific Publishing Company, 1982.

Fast, A.W. Article in *Principles and Practises of Pond Aquaculture* (J.E. Lannan, R.O. Smitherman, G. Tchobanoglous, editors); Oregon State University Press, 1990.

Kuroki, Dr. T. and R. Nogami. *Basic Koi Keeping* (various articles in *Nichirin* magazine), 1997–1998.

Kuroki, Dr. T. *Manual of Nishikigoi*, Shin Nippon Kyoiku Tosho Co. Ltd., 1990.

Kuroki, T. *Modern Nishikigoi: Basic Varieties and Unique Koi*, Shin Nippon Kyoiku Tosho Co. Ltd., 1986.

McDowell, A. (Editor). *The Practical Encyclopedia of Koi*, Salamander Books, 1989.

Michaels, V.K. *Carp Farming*, Fishing News Books, 1988.

Pillay, T.V.R. *Aquaculture: Principles and Practises*, Fishing News Books, 1990.

Pool, Dr. D. *The United Colours of Nishikigoi*, Nishikigoi International Ltd.

Tamadachi, M. *The Cult of Koi*. TFH Publications, 1990.

Wedermeyer, Gary A. *Fish Hatchery Management* (2nd edition). American Fisheries Society, Bethesda, Maryland, 2001.

Wheaton, F.W. *Aquaculture Engineering*. Kriegler Publishing, Florida, 1993.

Yamada, R. *Pond*, "Production Systems: Fertilization Practises in Warmwater Fish Ponds," article in *Principles and Practises of Pond Aquaculture*, J.E. Lannan, R.O. Smitherman, and G. Tchobanoglous (editors), Oregon State University Press, 1986.

Various articles in the following magazines: *Nichirin*, *Rinko*, *Aquarist and Pondkeeper*; *Koi SA*.

Acknowledgments

The authors would like to thank the following people for their support and assistance: Katsushi Takeda, Hiroshi Masuda, Susumu Shinoda, Masao Kata, and Inouye Toru, for many years of insight into Japanese koi culture; Dr. Liu Kai-Yuan and Dr. Mao-Lin Tsai of Taiwan (R.O.C.) for valuable lessons in koi breeding; Emiko Krupp for translation work; Hannes Uys Christie van Zyl and Khuthala Matinise of Cape Koi Aquarium, for providing material and assisting with the photo shoots; Christine Seegers at the Faculty of Veterinary Science, University of Pretoria, South Africa, for the original artwork of koi anatomy, and Dr. Anna Mouton for the micro-photography of parasites and the chromatophores; Chris Neaves, for assisting with writing the chapter on feeding; Dr. Nobuhiko Taniguchi and his team at the Laboratory of Population Genetic Informantics, Tohoku University, Sendai, for opening our minds to genetics; and Professor Boris Gomelsky at Kentucky State University, USA, and Dr. Hans Komen at Wegeningen University, Netherlands, for guiding us to a better understanding of their work on koi genetics; and Keith Rose of Hout Bay, South Africa, and Jim Pearce of Tetbury, England, for generously sponsoring some of the research that went into this book.

The authors would also like to thank *Nichirin* and *Rinko* magazines for supplying information and illustrative material. Yuko Shirako's staff at *Nichirin* in Beppu, Japan, helped to select material from the magazine's vast photo archive. Kiyoko Fujita, at the *Rinko* office in Tokyo, assisted with finding additional illustrative material and never failed to share our enthusiasm to track down obscure bits of information. Finally, we thank our family and friends, who tolerated our obsession to create a book that encapsulates all our knowledge, experience, and appreciation for koi.

Photographic credits

Copyright rests with the individuals and/or their agencies listed below: Left = l; center = c; right = r; bottom = b; top = t.

NHIL/DIS (photography by Digital Imaging Solutions for New Holland Image Library).

Original artwork on pages 23 and 29 by Christine Seegers, © Servaas de Kock and Ronnie Watt.

1	Servaas de Kock	49 (r)	*Nichirin*	74	Dave Bevan
2	Great Stock/Corbis/	50 (l,c)	*Nichirin*	75–84	NHIL/DIS
	Craig Lovell	50 (r)	*Rinko*	86	Servaas de Kock
4–5	NHIL/DIS	51	*Rinko*	87–92	NHIL/DIS
6–7	Dave Bevan	52 (l,r)	*Nichirin*	93	Dave Bevan
8–9	Dave Bevan	52 (c)	Servaas de Kock	94–101	NHIL/DIS
10–11	Great Stock/Corbis/	53 (l)	*Rinko*	102–103	Gallo
	Tom Wagner	53 (c,r)	*Nichirin*	104–107	Servaas de Kock
12	*Rinko*	54 (l,c)	*Nichirin*	110	Dave Bevan
14–15	Dave Bevan	54 (r)	*Rinko*	111	*Nichirin*
16–19	Servaas de Kock	55 (l,r)	*Rinko*	112	NHIL/DIS
20–21	Dave Bevan	55 (c)	Servaas de Kock	113	*Nichirin*
22	NHIL/DIS	56	*Nichirin*	114–115	NHIL/DIS
24 (t)	Dave Bevan	57 (l)	Servaas de Kock	116	Dave Bevan
24 (c)	Servaas de Kock	57 (r)	*Rinko*	117	NHIL/DIS
24 (b)	Servaas de Kock	57 (c)	*Nichirin*	118	Dave Bevan
25 (l)	Anna Mouton	58 (l,c)	*Nichirin*	120	NHIL/DIS
25 (r)	NHIL/DIS	58 (r)	*Rinko*	121	Nigel Hicks
26–27(t)	Dave Bevan	59 (l,c)	*Rinko*	122	Dave Bevan
27 (b)	Servaas de Kock	59 (r)	*Nichirin*	123	NHIL/DIS
28–30	Dave Bevan	60 (l,c)	*Rinko*	124–125	Great Stock/Masterfile/
31	Corbis	60 (r)	*Nichirin*		Carl Valiquet
32–33	Frantisek Staud	61 (l,r)	*Rinko*	126	Dave Bevan
34	Servaas de Kock	61 (c)	*Nichirin*	127	Dave Bevan
35	NHIL/DIS	62 (l)	*Rinko*	128	Gallo
36 (l,c)	*Nichirin*	62 (c)	*Nichirin*	129	Dave Bevan
36 (c)	*Nichirin*	62 (r)	Servaas de Kock	130	*Rinko*
36 (r)	*Rinko*	62 (t)	*Rinko*	131 (t)	Dave Bevan
37	*Nichirin*	63 (l)	*Nichirin*	131 (b)	Anna Mouton
38–39	Servaas de Kock	63 (c,r)	*Rinko*	13	Dave Bevan
41	*Nichirin*	64	Servaas de Kock	133	Anna Mouton
43	*Nichirin*	65 (l)	*Nichirin*	134 (l)	NHIL/DIS
44 (l,c)	*Nichirin*	65 (c,r)	*Rinko*	134 (r)	Dave Bevan
44 (r)	*Rinko*	66	*Nichirin*	135	Dave Bevan
45 (l)	*Nichirin*	67 (l,c)	*Nichirin*	136–139	NHIL/DIS
45 (c)	Servaas de Kock	67 (r)	*Rinko*	140–141	Great Stock/Corbis/
45 (r)	*Rinko*	68	*Nichirin*		Vince Streano
47 (t)	Servaas de Kock	69 (l,c)	*Rinko*	142–144	Servaas de Kock
47 (l)	*Rinko*	69 (r)	*Nichirin*	145	Dave Bevan
47 (c)	*Nichirin*	70–71	Great Stock/Corbis/	146–147	NHIL/DIS
47 (r)	*Rinko*		Michael S. Yamashita	148	Servaas de Kock
48	*Nichirin*	72	Corbis	149	Servaas de Kock
49 (l)	*Rinko*	73	NHIL/DIS	160	Dave Bevan